The Book of Acts

WILSON PAROSCHI

 **Pacific Press®**
Publishing Association

Nampa, Idaho | Oshawa, Ontario, Canada
www.pacificpress.com

Additional copies of this book can be purchased by calling toll-free 1-800-765-6955 or by visiting AdventistBookCenter.com.

Library of Congress Cataloging-in-Publication Data

Names: Paroschi, Wilson, author.
Title: The Book of Acts / Wilson Paroschi.
Description: Nampa : Pacific Press Publishing Association, 2018.
Identifiers: LCCN 2017058872 | ISBN 9780816363544 (pbk.)
Subjects: LCSH: Bible. Acts—Commentaries.
Classification: LCC BS2625.53 .P368 2018 | DDC 226.6/07—dc23
LC record available at https://lccn.loc.gov/2017058872

March 2018

Contents

Acknowledgments

I am writing this note in the middle of a major transition in my life. Though positive in many ways, it could in at least one aspect represent a great loss for me and my family, if not for the providential help of some church administrators in Brazil.

I would also like to express my sincere gratitude to three individuals who have stood by me in this and several other situations: To Pastor Paulo Martini, the president of Brazil Adventist University, Engenheiro Coelho (Centro Universitário Adventista de São Paulo, Engenheiro Coelho), the school I have proudly served for more than three decades; his commitment and unconditional support have strengthened me during all the years we have worked together. To Pastor Domingos J. de Sousa, the president of the Central Brazil Union; his openness, encouragement, and trust meant a lot to me even when it was a lost cause. And to Pastor Acílio Alves Filho, the president of the West São Paulo Conference—his personal involvement in this case, as much as his abiding friendship, which far exceeds church-related matters, has been a blessing to me.

Several others, including administrators and colleagues, participated in this process and, though not individually named here, are also much appreciated. To all of them, my heartfelt thanks.

INTRODUCTION

Acts

The Victory of the Gospel

He lived there two whole years at his own expense and welcomed all who come to him, proclaiming the kingdom of God and teaching about the Lord Jesus Christ with all boldness and without hindrance.
—Acts 28:30, 31, NRSV

Three crucial decades in world history. That is all it took. . . . In those thirty years it [the Christian movement] got sufficient growth and credibility to become the largest religion the world has ever seen and to change the lives of hundreds of millions of people. It has spread into every corner of the globe and has more than two billion putative adherents. It has had an indelible impact on civilization, on culture, on education, on medicine, on freedom and of course on the lives of countless people worldwide. And the seedbed for all this, the time when it took decisive root, was in these three decades. It all began with a dozen men and a handful of women: and then the Spirit came.[1]

Acts is an account of those years, which span from the resurrection of Jesus in A.D. 31 to the end of Paul's first Roman imprisonment in A.D. 62. The book—which has traditionally been ascribed to Luke, the "beloved physician" of Colossians 4:14 and a member of Paul's missionary team—must have been written shortly thereafter, for it stops the narrative at that point, implying that the apostle was set free at the end of his prison term (Acts 28:30, 31). This is exactly what can be inferred from Paul's later

7

writings (the pastoral epistles), which portray him as resuming his missionary activities (1 Timothy 1:3; Titus 1:5; 3:12; cf. Philemon 22) until he was arrested again and executed in Rome a few years later in A.D. 67 (2 Timothy 1:15–18; 4:6–8).

Those three decades were foundational because they witnessed the first developments of the church's identity within the socioreligious context of the day. Some of the most important issues the believers dealt with in that period were the time of Jesus' second coming, the character of Christian mission, the status of the Gentiles, and the role of faith in the plan of salvation.

But this time was not without struggle and tension, both external and internal. Though imbued with the Spirit, the apostolic church is not an example of purity and perfection— the ideal that future Christian generations should strive to reproduce. It is easy to romanticize the early church and think of this period as all flowers and sunshine—a period of peace, harmony, and impeccable piety. This skewed view of early Christianity goes back to the first centuries and is still embedded in the minds of many, as if "the church began with a golden age. . . , a time when the gospel was proclaimed and mighty works of power performed, when believers were all of one heart and soul in apostolic concord, and they shared all they had with one another."[2]

This perception is misleading, and Acts sets the record straight. We find that the early believers, including the apostles, were entangled with misconceptions, personal conflicts, prejudice, and other human difficulties. They were not infallible, and not all of their actions were right or proved to be a blessing for the church.

What they were able to accomplish in such a short period of time, however, is a perpetual testimony of how powerfully God can work when men and women, despite their limitations and failures, humble their hearts in prayer and "give themselves up to the control of . . . [the Holy] Spirit."[3] We should view Acts, therefore, not so much as the story of the apostles' missionary successes but rather as the story of God's mighty interventions through them in planting once and for all His saving flag in the post-Resurrection world, reclaiming humanity for Himself. God is definitely the main character of the narrative, and no one, not even Paul, had anything to boast about because it was all made possible through His infinite grace and power (cf. 1 Corinthians 15:9, 10).

This book is neither a commentary on Acts nor a reconstruction of the church's formative years. It is a supplement to the *Adult Sabbath School Bible Study Guide*, with the same title, and, as such, is focused on further discussion related to the lessons. Those readers who would like a more detailed understanding of Acts, the apostolic church, or Paul's life are invited to consider the recommended reading at the end of this volume. For an inspired and inspiring read, *The Acts of the Apostles*, by Ellen G. White, is particularly good.

Consider this

"The church is God's appointed agency for the salvation of men. It was organized for service, and its mission is to carry the gospel to the world. . . . The church is the repository of the riches of the grace of Christ; and through the church will eventually be made manifest, even to 'the principalities and powers in heavenly places,' the final and full display of the love of God."[4]

"The church, enfeebled and defective, needing to be reproved, warned, and counseled, is the only object upon earth upon which Christ bestows His supreme regard. The world is a workshop in which, through the cooperation of human and divine agencies, Jesus is making experiments by His grace and divine mercy upon human hearts."[5]

---

1. Michael Green, *Thirty Years That Changed the World: The Book of Acts for Today*, 2nd ed. (Grand Rapids, MI: Wm. B. Eerdmans, 2002), 7.

2. C. K. Robertson, *Conversations With Scripture: The Acts of the Apostles* (Harrisburg, PA: Morehouse, 2010), 18.

3. Ellen White, *The Acts of the Apostles* (Mountain View, CA: Pacific Press®, 1911), 49.

4. White, *The Acts of the Apostles*, 9.

5. Ellen White, *Counsels for the Church* (Mountain View, CA: Pacific Press®, 1957), 240.

CHAPTER 1

You Will Be My Witnesses

Acts 1

*"You will receive power when the Holy Spirit has come upon you;
and you will be my witnesses in Jerusalem, in all Judea and Samaria,
and to the ends of the earth."*
—Acts 1:8, NRSV

Modern TV series often finish one episode with a preview of the next one, and that episode usually opens with a brief review of the previous installment. Luke uses this approach when he previews the book of Acts in the closing paragraphs of his Gospel account. He reports Jesus' post-Resurrection appearances to the disciples, His final instructions to them, His promise of the Holy Spirit, and His departure to heaven (Luke 24:36–53). He then begins the book of Acts with a similar account (Acts 1:2–14). In Acts, however, Luke goes beyond a simple recounting of events and sets the perspective for what follows, including the disciples' failure to understand Jesus' mission, the promise of His return, and the plan for taking the gospel "to the ends of the earth" (verse 8, NRSV).

The restoration of Israel

According to Luke, the main issue the risen Christ dealt with during the forty days He stayed with the disciples was the nature of the kingdom of God (Acts 1:3). Up to that moment, they had not been able to make sense of the Cross and, despite all Jesus' efforts to warn them about His fate (Matthew 16:21), none of them were expecting Him to die (cf. verses 22, 23). They expected a literal kingship on earth, not the salvation of humankind and the reinstatement of God's spiritual kingship on earth (Matthew 4:17, 23). When they left everything to follow Jesus, they believed He was the Messiah (John 1:41). In their minds, however, they viewed the Messiah as a warrior king; one who would deliver them from the Romans and restore Israel to its past glory.

This notion was typical of first-century Judaism. Though the term *Messiah* occurs only twice in the Old Testament (Daniel 9:25, 26), the concept of a Messianic figure as an agent of deliverance is inescapable. Sometimes the Messiah is quietly presented as one who would restore the Edenic condition that was lost at the Fall (Isaiah 11:6–9) or as a new Moses who would lead Israel into a second and greater exodus (Isaiah 51:9–11). In the case of Moses, his own prophecy clearly shows he understood that a new prophet was coming (Deuteronomy 18:15–19).

When it comes to explicit references, the most prominent Messianic concepts are those of the Davidic King who would establish His throne and rule forever (Psalm 2:6–9) and of the Suffering Servant who would be rejected and die for the sins of the people (Isaiah 52:13–53:12). Though such prophecies seem contradictory, they simply indicate the two consecutive phases of the Messiah's work: first He would suffer, and then He would become king (cf. Luke 17:24, 25; 24:25–27, 44–47).

Unfortunately, the Jews allowed the idea of a kingly Messiah, who would bring political deliverance, to obscure the notion of a suffering Messiah, who would bring spiritual liberation. Of course, the Messiah's kingship was not political in the secular sense of the word because it was concerned with the eradication of sin and the reestablishment of God's kingship in the universe. This is why Jesus said to Pilate, "My kingdom is not of this world" (John 18:36, NKJV).

So it is not difficult to understand why the Jews were confused about the Messiah. Since the fall of Jerusalem to Babylon in 586 B.C., they had rarely enjoyed political freedom. Even when they did—during the Hasmonean period (142–63 B.C.)—the occupants of the throne were of Levite lineage and not descendants of David, meaning they had no traditional right to rule (cf. Genesis 49:10; 2 Samuel 7:16).

Due to their successful leadership during the Maccabean revolt against the Seleucids (beginning in 167 B.C.), they appropriated not only the kingship but also the high priesthood. Their procurement of the priesthood was illegitimate because they were not from the house of Zadok, who was a priest in David's time (2 Samuel 15:24–29). It was Zadok's descendants who were given a monopoly on the priesthood (1 Kings 2:26, 27, 35; 1 Chronicles 27:17), and the combination of king and high priest on the part of the Hasmonean family only intensified the desire by various orthodox Jews for a Davidic King. These circumstances led the Essenes, a conservative Jewish group, to leave Jerusalem and settle in the desert, near the Dead Sea. Here they waited in anticipation of the coming priestly Messiah who would restore the Zadokite priesthood.

Since the Babylonian exile, the Jews had longed more than ever for a kingly Messiah. The continuing oppression and humiliation by foreign powers fueled their nationalistic ideals and distorted their Messianic expectation. This explains why Jesus avoided the term *Messiah* altogether and warned the disciples not to share His Messianic identity with others (Mark 8:27–30). On only three occasions did Jesus explicitly acknowledge being the Messiah: in Samaria, outside the Jewish borders (John 4:25, 26); to the Twelve, only a few months before His death (Matthew 16:13–20); and before the Sanhedrin, the very day He died (Mark 14:60–63). He understood that it was unwise to use the term because of its political and self-serving connotations.

This is illustrated in the feeding of the five thousand (John 6:1–15). That the crowd wanted to make Jesus king shows they thought of Him in Messianic fashion, the same short-term earthly interests about the Messiah that prevailed in contemporary Judaism. They saw Him as one who could lead a revolt against the Romans, feed the troops, heal the wounded, and free the land from its hateful invaders (verses 14, 15). They only wanted to use Him to pursue their own ends (verse 26), so He slipped away into the hills.

Even the Jewish religious leaders suffered from the same misconception. Aware of Jesus' charisma and Messianic reputation among the people, they feared He would worsen their political situation by attracting the fury of the Romans and thus bring the destruction of Jerusalem (John 11:47–50; 19:12). Since, in their view, Jesus did not have Messianic credentials, they considered Him an impostor, like several others in recent Jewish history (Acts 5:36, 37).[1]

It is not surprising, then, that the disciples would nurture wrong ideas about Jesus. They sincerely believed Jesus was the Messiah of Israel and were concerned about which of them would sit on either side of Him in the kingdom (Mark 10:35–37). Thus, when Jesus died, their disappointment could not have been greater. Their dreams of glory were shattered, and with great sorrow, they cried, "We had hoped that he was the one who was going to redeem Israel" (Luke 24:21, NIV). The Roman yoke remained, and "their expectation of a Messiah who was to take His throne and kingly power," Ellen White writes, "had been misleading."[2]

Jesus' death was a devastating blow to the disciples, but the Resurrection raised their political expectations to an unprecedented level. Finally, the long-awaited Messianic kingdom would be established! But their Acts 1 question (Acts 1:6) about restoring the kingdom of Israel shows they were still confused. Even after the Resurrection, they continued to think politically.

In His reply to their kingdom query, Jesus intentionally left the issue unsettled. He did not reject the premise behind the disciples' question of an imminent kingdom, neither did He accept it. He only reminded them that the time of God's actions belongs to God Himself and, as such, is inaccessible to humans (Acts 1:7). It was in this context that Jesus must have explained to them once again the real nature of His Messianic mission (Luke 24:44). They were familiar with the prophecies, but their minds had been preconditioned to think of the Messiah as an earthly ruler. Now they were able to have a fresh understanding of what the prophets had written and see the kingdom in a new light—a light shed from the empty tomb (verse 46).

The disciples' mission

What came next were Jesus' instructions regarding the ultimate purpose of the disciples' calling (Acts 1:8). It is clear that chronological speculation about the Messianic kingdom (cf. verses 6, 7) was to be replaced with bearing witness in Jerusalem, Judea, Samaria, and all over the world. This huge shift in God's plan for Israel encapsulated four important points concerning the disciples' mission.

1. *The gift of the Spirit.* In a striking passage, Josephus states that in the siege of Jerusalem in A.D. 70 there were so many crosses outside the walls that there could hardly be room for more. The reference is to the hundreds of Jews who were caught and mercilessly crucified every day while trying to escape the horrors of famine and despair inside the city.[3] In another passage, he describes how in 4 B.C. Quintilius Varus, the Roman governor of Syria, crucified two thousand Jews who were fighting for freedom from the Roman yoke.[4]

There were thousands of other crucifixions during this period in history, so it is reasonable to ask, What is it that sets Jesus' cross apart from all others? The answer is the activity of the Holy Spirit. The Spirit is the real power behind the gospel (1 Corinthians 2:12, 13), and without Him, Jesus' cross would have been only one among many in the ancient world. It would have had no redemptive significance. No one would be attracted to it. There would be no conviction of sin, no conversion, no transformation of heart, and no sanctified life. The church would not exist, God's kingdom would not be established, and no one would be inspired to preach the gospel.

The mission of the disciples, therefore, was entirely dependent on the Spirit's intervention. This is why Pentecost was necessary. It was Jesus' victory on the cross that granted God the authority to send the Spirit in full measure as never before, and it was the Spirit who, through apostolic preaching, would reveal all the benefits of the cross to a lost world (verses 7–13).

2. *The role of witness.* Jesus chose twelve disciples to work with Him and witness His ministry (Matthew 11:1). In just a few short years, they observed miracles, listened to sermons,

and marveled at His love. Above all others, they were qualified to give a firsthand account of what they had seen, heard, and experienced during their time with the Master (1 John 1:1–3). Jesus called them "apostles" (from the Greek *apostellō*, "to send") (Luke 6:13) and commissioned them to share the gospel, which is the good news that forgiveness and salvation are available through Jesus Christ, and only through Him, to all who believe (Acts 4:12).

They still had much to learn about the plan of salvation, and the forty days Jesus spent with them after the Resurrection were crucial for their understanding that His death was not in conflict with His Messianic identity. He deflected their concern about the timing of the establishment of His kingdom, although the two angels' promise of Jesus' second coming (Acts 1:11) and Pentecost itself (Acts 2) must have naturally strengthened their anticipation of its nearness. A careful reading of Acts shows that it took time for the disciples to reconcile their hope of Jesus' soon return with the notion of a worldwide mission. As it turns out, it was Paul, not any of the Twelve, who deployed the first systematic efforts to evangelize the Gentile world.

3. *The plan of the mission.* The disciples were to witness first in Jerusalem, then in Judea and Samaria, and finally to "the ends of the earth," an expression taken from Isaiah 49:6 that simply means the whole world. It was a progressive plan that began in Jerusalem, the center of Jewish religious life and the place where Jesus had been condemned and crucified. Judea and Samaria were neighboring areas where Jesus had also ministered (John 3:22; 4:1–42), and familiarity with His life and teachings would likely make the people more receptive to the gospel message. In the Samaritans' case, there were many points of contact between their religion and that of the Jews. They shared the hope of a Messiah, whom they called *Taheb* ("Restorer")—a prophetic figure like Moses (cf. Deuteronomy 18:15–18) who would bring about a new order of things, pray for the guilty, and save them.[5] But the disciples were not to limit themselves to Palestine. The scope of their mission was

worldwide, fulfilling God's promise to Abraham (Genesis 12:3; 18:18; 22:18). The spread of the gospel, as recorded in Acts, clearly reflects the plan outlined in Acts 1:8.

4. *The orientation of the mission.* The centrifugal pattern of the disciples' mission was exactly opposite that of ancient Israel. In the Old Testament, surrounding nations were to be attracted to God through Israel. There was no explicit direction for Israel to *take* God to the nations. The mission pattern was centripetal, as evidenced by Solomon's dedicatory prayer for the temple, "Come and see what God has done" (1 Kings 8:41–43, ESV).[6] The story of Jonah, and a few other exceptions, do not invalidate this general rule (Isaiah 2:2–4).

Now the strategy was different. By renouncing theocracy (John 19:14, 15),[7] national Israel would no longer be the agent through which God's saving plan would be conveyed to the

Acts and the mission plan

1:1–7:60	**Witnessing in Jerusalem**
1:1–2:47	The beginning of the church
3:1–7:60	The church in Jerusalem
8:1–11:18	**Witnessing in Judea and Samaria**
8:1–9:43	The church begins to expand
10:1–11:18	The inauguration of the Gentile mission
11:19–28:31	**Witnessing to the ends of the earth**
11:19–14:28	The mission in Cyprus and south Galatia
15:1–35	The discussion concerning the Gentiles in the church
16:6–18:17	The mission in Macedonia and Achaia
18:18–20:3	The mission in Asia
21:1–28:31	Paul's arrest and imprisonment in Caesarea and Rome

world; the messengers would be those who believed in Jesus, irrespective of their ethnicity (cf. 1 Peter 2:9, 10). It was a seismic missional change. Jerusalem was still the center; but rather

17

than remaining and building roots there, the disciples were expected to move out to the uttermost ends of the earth.

Concluding remarks

Upon the completion of the instructions to the Twelve, it was time for Jesus to return to heaven and give way to the Holy Spirit. While His followers readied themselves for Pentecost, they were together in Jerusalem, waiting in prayer for that great event (Acts 1:14). A new age in God's redemptive plan would soon begin, an age in which the good news of the gospel would be taken to the entire world in preparation for the complete establishment of God's kingship (Matthew 24:14). The long-awaited Messianic kingdom, whose legitimacy was vindicated at the cross, would finally be revealed in the fullness of its glory and power (Luke 21:27). The Messiah would reign forever (Revelation 11:15).

---

1. See Lester L. Grabbe, *An Introduction to First Century Judaism: Jewish Religion and History in the Second Temple Period* (Edinburgh: T&T Clark, 1996), 53–72.

2. Ellen White, *The Desire of Ages* (Oakland, CA: Pacific Press®, 1898), 799.

3. Josephus, *The Jewish War* 5.11.1.

4. Josephus, *The Antiquities of the Jews* 17.10.10.

5. See Louis H. Feldman, *Josephus's Interpretation of the Bible* (Berkeley, CA: University of California Press, 1998), 397n47.

6. George W. Peters, *A Biblical Theology of Missions* (Chicago: Moody Press, 1972), 21.

7. See White, *The Desire of Ages*, 737, 738.

Pentecost

From the time of Creation, the Holy Spirit has always been active on earth (Genesis 1:2). As the main agency through which God works, His presence in the Old Testament is prominent and often revealed in notable ways. The Spirit gives life (Job 33:4; Psalm 104:30), strives with humanity (Genesis 6:3), instructs people (Nehemiah 9:20, 30; Job 32:8), rests on the faithful (Genesis 41:38; Numbers 27:18), and empowers Israel's leaders to do God's work (Numbers 11:25).

Yet the Spirit's activity also involves a future aspect, and Jesus refers to Him as having been promised by the Father (Luke 24:49; Acts 1:4). In several Old Testament passages, the Spirit is presented as the gift of the new age that, introduced by the Messiah (Isaiah 11:1–5; 42:1–9; 61:1–11), would bring salvation for both Israel (Isaiah 32:12–20) and the world (Joel 2:28–32).

As part of his preparatory ministry, John the Baptist announced baptism with the Spirit as a function of the coming Messiah (Luke 3:16). Jesus would later bestow the Spirit on the disciples in His last days with them (John 20:22), proving that the Spirit was already at work during the time of His ministry. But the official inauguration, however, would have to wait until His exaltation in heaven (John 7:39; Acts 2:33); but when the time was right, the Holy Spirit assumed His role in a powerful and dramatic fashion. Pentecost launched the church in its worldwide mission (John 16:7).

According to Acts 2:4, the gift of the Spirit was manifested in the gift of tongues. As incredible as this was, the New Testament does not consider it to be the typical endowment of the Spirit. In fact, there are only four other references to the gift of tongues in the New Testament: twice in the book of Acts (10:45, 46; 19:6) and twice in 1 Corinthians (12:10; 14:1–24). Interestingly, 1 Corinthians designates tongues as one of several gifts of the Spirit and further states that no believer has all of the gifts. Paul's rhetorical question "Do all speak in tongues?" (1 Corinthians 12:30, ESV) begs an answer of No, and the next verses refer to greater gifts, such as love and prophecy (1 Corinthians 12:31–14:5).

The tongues at Pentecost, apparently restricted to the apostles and Peter's words in Acts 2:38, 39, refer quite generally to the gift of the Spirit, not to the gift of tongues in particular. Furthermore, the gift of tongues had a specific purpose: to launch the church's world mission. If the apostles were to cross borders and reach the ends of the earth with the gospel, they would need to speak the languages of their listeners. This is exactly what happened to Paul (1 Corinthians 14:18), and he insisted that tongues were useless unless they were clear in purpose (verse 22) and intelligible (verses 6–9).

That the tongues of Pentecost were existing foreign languages is evident for the following reasons: (1) the term "tongue" (*glōssa*) in Acts 2:4, 11 is explained in verses 6 and 8 as *dialektos*, the vernacular "*language* of a nation or a region"[2] (cf. Acts 1:19; 21:40; 22:2; 26:14); (2) the crowd was amazed, not because they were hearing an ecstatic utterance but because they could hear the apostles in their own native language (Acts 2:6, 8); and (3) the appended list of nationalities (verses 9–11) is intended to exemplify the languages that were represented there, which is corroborated by the pronoun "our" (*hēmeteros*) in verse 11. The most natural way of taking Luke's account of Pentecost is that the tongues spoken that day were the vernacular languages of the people present.

It is estimated that in the first century A.D. there were eight to ten million Jews in the world and that up to 60 percent of them lived outside Palestine, mostly in regions under the influence of Greek culture. They were known as Hellenistic Jews (cf. Acts 6:1; 9:29).

It was not uncommon, however, for many such Jews to move to Palestine at a certain point in life. Nevertheless, they were still foreigners, and most of them could not speak Aramaic, which was the language of Palestinian Jews at that time. In Jerusalem, they must have lived in their own districts where they had their own synagogues (cf. Acts 6:9; 9:29) and guesthouses for pilgrims and foreign visitors. The so-called Theodotos synagogue, whose inscription was found in 1914 south of the Temple Mount, was certainly one of those.

There is no question that most converts at Pentecost were resident Hellenistic Jews (Acts 2:5) who could hear the gospel in their mother language. The gift of tongues was initially aimed at them as the church was prepared to direct its missionary efforts toward the Gentile world. The gift was also to be a sign for the Palestinian Jews who witnessed the scene and were not acquainted with such languages. Some observers were perplexed and honestly inquired about the meaning of what was going on (verse 12); others reacted with skepticism and even mockery by accusing the apostles of drunkenness (verse 13).

The meaning of Pentecost

These reactions prompted Peter to address the people regarding the significance of the tongues phenomenon. His speech, abridged by Luke, consists of three main parts; the first of which describes the coming of the Spirit as the fulfillment of an Old Testament prophecy (Joel 2:28–32).

Joel's prophecy was about the future age of salvation (verse 32), which would be characterized by several signs in the natural world and an abundant outpouring of the Spirit (verses 28–31). By interpreting Pentecost in this light, Peter intended to stress the historical relevance of the moment. There is, however, an important difference in the way he quotes Joel. Instead of Joel's introductory "afterward" (verse 28), which pointed quite generally to the future, Peter says, "In the last days" (Acts 2:17, NIV), indicating that the final act in the great drama of salvation had just begun (cf. 2 Corinthians 6:2). What would come next was "the great and glorious day of the Lord" (Acts 2:20, NIV), also understood as a day of judgment (Zechariah 14:1; 2 Peter 3:10).

This is not, of course, a full description of the last-day events but an evidence of the high sense of urgency that distinguished the early church. They did not know when the end would come, but they were convinced it was imminent.

The second part of the speech focuses on the recent events of Jesus' life, death, and resurrection (Acts 2:22–32). Focusing on the Resurrection as the decisive element in the gospel story,

Peter forcefully makes the case that Jesus was not an ordinary man. As the Messiah, He could not be detained by death.

Peter graphically describes the Resurrection as "loosing the pangs of death" (verse 24, ESV). The term for "pangs" is *ōdin*, which literally means "birth pains," while the verb *lyō* should probably be understood as "to bring to an end." The idea, then, is that death was in labor and unable to retain its child. By resurrecting Jesus, God Himself stepped in and helped to relieve the pain.[3]

Finally, in the third part of the speech (verses 33–36), Peter goes back to the issue of tongues, explaining the outpouring of the Spirit in light of Jesus' exaltation to the right hand of God, which is a position of honor and authority (1 Peter 3:22). The exaltation did not grant Jesus a status He did not have before (John 1:1–3; 17:5) but instead signified the Father's formal recognition of Jesus' prerogative as Lord and Messiah (Acts 2:36).

This brings us to an important theme in Scripture: the cosmic conflict between good and evil. It is customary to refer to Pentecost as "the most important event" recorded in Acts;[4] one that sanctioned faith in Jesus Christ and united His followers under the fellowship of the Spirit. While this is correct, within the broader context of redemptive history, Pentecost was the beginning of God's wholesale assault on Satan's kingdom. The Spirit could not come if Jesus was not exalted (John 7:39), and Jesus would not be exalted if He had not triumphed on the cross (John 17:4, 5). In other words, Jesus' exaltation was the necessary condition for the Spirit's arrival because it signified God's approval of Jesus' accomplishments on the cross (Philippians 2:8, 9; Revelation 5:12), including the defeat of the one who had usurped the rule of this world (Revelation 12:9).

Since this is a moral universe, the emergence of sin cast a deep shadow on God's character and rule, making Him appear somewhat responsible for it. This made Jesus' death necessary, not only to save humanity but also to vindicate God and expose Satan as a fraud (Colossians 2:15). In fact, there is a causal relationship between these two in the sense that the former could not have happened without the latter. The Cross vindicated God's rule of this world (Revelation 5:5, 12, 13) and His right to draw Satan's captives back to Himself (John 3:14; 12:32; cf. Acts 5:31, 32; Revelation 12:10). Thus, Jesus could say to the Father in anticipation of His death: "I glorified you on earth by finishing the work that you gave me to do" (John 17:4, NRSV).

Gift of tongues or interpretation?

Based on Acts 2:6, 8, it has been argued that the gift at Pentecost was of interpretation, not of tongues. The passage (verse 6), however, makes it clear that the crowd heard the apostles "speak" (*laleō*) in their own native languages, as opposed to being the ones who heard in their native languages.

It is important to notice that they had not yet come to faith, nor received the Spirit (verses 38–41). It was the apostles who were "filled with the Holy Spirit" and who "began to speak in other tongues" (verse 4, ESV). The crowd's reaction also confirms this. How could they have been "amazed and astonished" (verse 7, ESV) that it was Galileans who were speaking, rather than foreigners who could have learned such languages elsewhere, if the gift was one of interpretation?

The moment Jesus died, bringing His earthly mission to its expected end (John 12:27; cf. John 3:16, 17; 10:10), was in fact a moment of glory, both for Himself and for the Father (John 13:31; cf. 12:28). To human eyes, the Son of God hanging on the cross could be viewed as a sign of defeat and shame. In terms of the cosmic conflict, however, it signified the supreme triumph of God; a victory that allowed Him to regain moral control of the universe and carry out His saving activities (Romans 3:25, 26). This is why the age of salvation was still future to the Old Testament prophets, and as soon as Jesus' sacrifice was officially acknowledged in heaven, the Spirit came to launch that age.

Concluding remarks

Due to the devastating effects of sin, human nature became utterly depraved, losing the power and the disposition to resist evil.[5] It is only through the Holy Spirit that sinners can be convinced of sin, righteousness, and judgment (John 16:8–11) and can turn their hearts to God (1 Corinthians 12:3). "It is the Spirit that makes effectual what has been wrought out by the world's Redeemer."[6] The New Testament's intense focus on missionary activity was not centered in Jerusalem and the temple; it expanded to the world beyond. The triumph of the Cross was the foundation of the coming of the Spirit, the baptism of the Spirit, and the gospel going to the world.

There is an interesting episode in which Jesus was charged with collusion with evil because of His supernatural activities (Matthew 12:24). In His answer, He said, "How can someone enter a strong man's house and plunder his goods, unless he first binds the strong man? Then indeed he may plunder his house" (verse 29, ESV). This parabolic statement conveys an essential truth: no one tries to rob the house of a strong man without first neutralizing him. In Jesus' ministry, the age of salvation was already at work (Luke 4:18–21). When He cast out demons or forgave sins, He was defying Satan and releasing his captives (Luke 10:17, 18). Yet it was the Cross that would give Jesus the final authority to do that (John 14:31; Colossians 2:13–15). When He died, Satan was bound forever. It was now time to plunder and devastate his kingdom. At Pentecost, the Spirit came for that purpose and the initial result (the firstfruits) could not have been better.

The infant church went from 120 to more than 3,000 believers (Acts 1:15; 2:41). Soon they would be about 5,000 (Acts 4:4), then a great multitude of men and women (Acts 5:14), and the numbers kept mounting (Acts 6:7). Yet statistics are not everything. In fact, nothing could be more deceptive than trying to measure church growth by merely counting baptisms. The early church was committed to the advancement of God's kingdom (Acts 8:12; 19:8; 28:23), not simply to baptizing. They were not driven by numbers; they were driven by a high sense of duty in response to Jesus' victory on the cross. The world was working under new rules.

1. Norman H. Cliff, *Courtyard of the Happy Way* (Evesham, UK: Arthur James, 1977), 120.

2. Frederick William Danker, ed., *A Greek-English Lexicon of the New Testament and Other Early Christian Literature*, 3rd ed. (Chicago: University of Chicago Press, 2000), 232; emphasis in original.

3. Gerhard Freidrich and Gerhard Kittel, eds., *Theological Dictionary of the New Testament*, vol. 9, trans. Geoffrey W. Bromiley (Grand Rapids, MI: Wm. B. Eerdmans, 1974), 673.

4. V. George Shillington, *The New Testament in Context: A Literary and Theological Textbook* (New York: T&T Clark, 2008), 133.

5. Ellen White, *Patriarchs and Prophets* (Battle Creek, MI: Review and Herald®, 1890), 53.

6. Ellen White, *The Desire of Ages* (Oakland, CA: Pacific Press®, 1898), 671.

CHAPTER 3

Life in the Early Church
Acts 2:42-5:42

Every day they continued to meet together in the temple courts. They broke bread in their homes and ate together with glad and sincere hearts, praising God and enjoying the favor of all the people.
—Acts 2:46, NIV

October 22, 1844, is well known among Adventists as the day of the Great Disappointment. Led by William Miller and his associates, thousands of North American Protestants became convinced through the study of Scripture that Jesus would come back on that day. Excitement swept through the ranks of the Millerite movement—"the blessed hope" of Jesus' return, as Paul describes it (Titus 2:13), was finally coming to fulfillment.

As the day approached, many faithful Millerites left their crops unharvested; others closed their stores or resigned their positions. In camp meetings, scores confessed their faults and stepped forward for prayer. Large sums were donated so that the poor could settle their debts and be ready to meet their Savior. As one author describes it, "The sense of apocalyptic time left derelict any long-range earthly concerns."[1]

With the early church, it was no different. Persuaded that the outpouring of the Spirit and thousands of conversions at Pentecost signaled the establishment of the Messianic kingdom, they sold everything they had, developed a common purse, and dedicated themselves to learning and fellowship. It is difficult to fault their zeal for the kingdom, but a growing challenge loomed on the horizon—living in a state of perpetual alert became problematic. For this reason, God initiated a

28

course correction that kept the church united and conscious of its worldwide mission.

The nearness concept

The Bible emphasizes that Jesus is coming soon (Hebrews 10:25, 37; James 5:8; Revelation 3:11; 22:12, 20; cf. Matthew 24:45–49; Luke 12:35–40). Since two thousand years have passed and He has not yet come, how is this emphasis to be understood?

There are at least two possible explanations. The first is the shortness and uncertainty of human life. No one knows how long he or she will live, and eighty or even ninety years seem brief, especially in view of eternity. As Moses properly said, "The years of our life . . . are soon gone, and we fly away" (Psalm 90:10, ESV). This is why, when it comes to salvation, the only time we can count on is the present (cf. Acts 22:16; Hebrews 3:7, 8, 13, 15; 4:6, 7). The past is gone, and the future may never come. Procrastination is a tragic mistake of eternal proportions.

The second explanation for the sense of nearness is that from God's perspective "one day is as a thousand years, and a thousand years as one day" (2 Peter 3:8, ESV). Peter's point is that God cannot be confined to our own understanding of time, so no one can judge Him based on human standards. The fact that Jesus has yet to return is not evidence that the promise has failed or that God's plans have been changed. On the contrary, from the human standpoint, the waiting time is but an indication of God's saving patience (verse 9). But it is not a patience that lasts forever. In His sovereign plan, God has set a time when Jesus will return and the present order of things will come to an end (Mark 13:32; cf. Acts 3:19–21; 17:30, 31).

Sense of urgency
As noted in chapter 1, when asked by the disciples about when He would inaugurate His kingdom (Acts 1:6), the risen Jesus

gave no direct answer (verse 7). By not explicitly contradicting the assumption of nearness, however, He could have been understood as reaffirming it—the only conditions being the coming of the Spirit and the preaching of the gospel to the whole world (verse 8). The angels' promise right after the ascension, assuring the disciples of Jesus' visible return (verses 9–11), could also be taken as indirect support of the idea that the time would be rather short.

From today's perspective, it seems obvious that the mission Jesus left with the disciples would require time. Two thousand years have slipped by, and the work is still not finished; but from the disciples' perspective, the outlook changes. Acquainted as they were with the Old Testament evangelistic pattern, in which the nations would flock to Jerusalem to hear the Word of God, and convinced that salvation could take place only within the limits of the Abrahamic covenant, it is not difficult to see that, for them, the conditions of Acts 1:8 had been met.

At Pentecost, they received the Spirit and shared the gospel with the whole world. No, they had not left Jerusalem, but the world had come to them (Acts 2:5, 9–11). This was in full harmony with what they knew about evangelism (cf. Matthew 8:11, 12; 10:5, 6; Mark 11:17), no matter how narrow the concept. The fact that those who were baptized at Pentecost were all Jews and proselytes (i.e., Jewish converts) was not a problem either, as according to the traditional Jewish understanding salvation could be granted only to those who were faithful to Abraham's covenant, in which circumcision and adherence to the Law played a central role (cf. Acts 11:3; 15:1, 5; Galatians 2:11–14). For them, the only thing lacking was Jesus' return.

At this point, it is worth noting that the same mistake would be repeated by Sabbatarian Adventists in the aftermath of the Millerite movement. Their mentality of world evangelism underwent progressive changes during the first fifty years of the Advent movement. At first under the assumption that the door of grace had been closed to the world (1844–1850), they felt compelled to preach only to those who had accepted the Millerite message. From 1850 to 1874, with an attitude reminiscent of the early church, they believed that preaching the third angel's message throughout the United States constituted the gospel to the entire world. Strange as this seems, they felt justified in this position because the country was composed of people from nearly every nation around the world.

During the next fifteen years (1874–1889), they would send some missionaries overseas but initially only to Christian nations where Protestantism had a strong presence. It was only after 1890 that the Seventh-day Adventist Church made significant efforts to reach all nations and all peoples, irrespective of their religious background.[2]

Going back to the first century now, a careful reading of Acts shows that the post-Pentecost church lived with a daily expectation of Jesus' return. First, there was a complete detachment from material goods and a readiness to share belongings with one another (Acts 2:45; 4:34–37). Sensing that time was short, an immediate pooling of resources seemed prudent, so they began to sell their properties and live from a common purse, according to their individual needs. "There was no need to take thought for the morrow since there would not be one."[3]

The second evidence was the fact that they remained rooted in Jerusalem and centered on the temple, which, according to the prophet Malachi, would be the focal point of the imminent consummation (Malachi 3:1). To some extent, Jesus' mysterious statement about destroying and rebuilding the temple (Mark 14:58) could somehow have fueled hope of a new religious order to be installed by the Messiah. It was only years later that the apostles understood that Jesus was referring to His resurrection (John 2:22).

The third evidence of their belief in the imminence of Jesus' return was the daily observance of the Lord's Supper (Acts 2:46; 5:42). As an antitype of the Passover and the most important annual feast of the Jewish calendar, the Lord's Supper points back to the cross, where Jesus, the Passover Lamb, was crucified (1 Corinthians 11:23–26). But a statement from Jesus also links it to the future, to the Messianic banquet that takes place at His return (Matthew 26:29; Revelation 19:7–9). In observing this service together on a daily basis, the early believers found a meaningful way to express their faith that Jesus would return soon.

Not all of this, however, proved to be a blessing to the church. The pooling of goods, though effective in helping the poor, soon became a problem. It impoverished the Judean church (cf. Romans 15:26; Galatians 2:10), which became dependent on the generosity of Gentile believers (cf. Acts 11:29; 2 Corinthians 9:1, 2, 12–14), leaving them unable to sponsor world evangelism. All of this shifted an undue burden onto the Gentile churches (Acts 13:1–3; 15:35, 36; 2 Corinthians 11:8, 9).

Such communal life does not seem to have lasted long and is not supported by any of the New Testament letters. On the contrary, when faced with a slight movement in that direction, Paul's reaction was rather strong (cf. 2 Thessalonians 3:6–12). Though the underlying premise of communal life was laudable, it was short lived, and Christian benevolence quickly became the norm for sacrificial living (Ephesians 4:28). For today's Christians, detachment from material things will be expected from God's people just before the Second Coming; but for the early church with a world mission to fulfill, it represented a step backward.

The second problem with communal life is the illusion that the church's mission had been achieved at Pentecost. The apostles continued to bear witness for Jesus in Jerusalem, but none of them moved more than a few dozen miles away. And when they did, it was not to lay the ground for new evangelistic work but to check on what others had done (Acts 8:14–25) or to shepherd those who had already been reached (Acts 9:32–43).

Even the episode involving Cornelius was initiated by God (Acts 10), highlighting the limited scope of evangelistic urgency in the nascent Christian church. It was only in the context of persecution, led by the unconverted Paul (Saul), that some believers crossed the Palestinian borders and embraced world mission (Acts 8:4–8, 26–35; 11:19–21).

Life in the Early Church

Teaching and fellowship

In his description of church life in Jerusalem, Luke states that believers "devoted themselves to the apostles' teaching and to fellowship, to the breaking of bread and to prayer" (Acts 2:42, NIV). Interpreters have noted that the four items mentioned here appear in two basic groupings: teaching and fellowship,[4] and the latter includes the breaking of bread and prayer. According to verse 46, teaching was primarily in the temple, and fellowship was in private homes.

The temple court was surrounded on two sides by magnificent roofed porches that were frequently used for rabbinic instruction. When Jesus taught in the temple, He likely made use of such porches (Luke 19:47), as did the apostles (Acts 3:11). In that tradition, believers devoted themselves to the apostles' teaching. Despite some confusion regarding the time of the Second Coming, the gift of the Spirit did not lead them to a contemplative religion but rather led them to an intense learning process under the apostles. The apostolic leaders were authoritative guardians of Jesus' life and teaching, and their work was authenticated by many signs and wonders (Acts 2:43; 5:12). Soon they would be accused by the Jewish authorities of filling Jerusalem with their doctrines (Acts 5:28).

Closely linked to teaching was spiritual fellowship. This distinctive mark of early Christian piety saw believers meeting in the temple and also in their homes, where they shared meals, celebrated the Lord's Supper, and prayed (Acts 2:42, 46; 5:42; cf. Acts 12:12). The meals, called love (Greek: *agapē*) feasts (Jude 12), were regular evening dinners that were given a religious connotation. Judaism had several religious meals, with Passover being one of them, but the practice of the early church may have had its origin in Jesus' post-Resurrection meals with the disciples (Acts 10:41; cf. Luke 24:30, 41, 42). The Lord's Supper had been instituted in the context of a domestic Jewish religious meal (Mark 14:22–25), and it continued to be observed in a meal setting (cf. 1 Corinthians 11:20–34). By having such daily celebrations, the early Christians expressed their hope in Jesus' soon return, when His fellowship with them would be restored in the Messianic kingdom (Matthew 26:29; 1 Corinthians 11:26).

Private homes played a key role in the early church's life. Publicly, believers still attended the temple's daily ceremonies (Acts 3:1) and on Sabbaths were presumably in the synagogues with fellow Jews (James 2:2; cf. *episynagōgē* in Hebrews 10:25).[5] The distinctive elements of Christian devotion, however, were performed in "home churches" (Greek: *ekklēsia kat'oikon*, which literally means "church in home") (Romans 16:5; 1 Corinthians 16:19; cf. Romans 16:10, 11, 15, 23).

In the years following the destruction of the Jerusalem temple in A.D. 70, the measures taken by rabbinic leaders to exclude Jewish Christians from synagogues caused the home churches to remain the only Christian places for religious services. Among Gentile Christians, this process happened much faster (cf. Acts 17:4–7; 18:5–8). The worship liturgy, however, continued to be based on that of the synagogue. Besides the love feasts and the Lord's Supper, other activities performed in home churches included praying, singing, studying the Word, sharing experiences (Colossians 3:16), and preaching the gospel (Acts 5:42; 28:30, 31).

Concluding remarks

In His post-Resurrection instructions to the disciples, Jesus left two legacies that have to be kept in perfect harmony: the expectation of His soon return and a worldwide mission. Expectation conveys a sense of urgency. Mission presupposes time. Without the former, there would be no preparation for the Second Coming or motivation for mission. Without the latter, there would be fanaticism and idle contemplation. This explains, at least in part, what happened to the early church. Though pooling resources for the common good served the early believers well, it eventually became an impediment to the growth of the gospel.

It has been said that we should be ready for Jesus' return today but work as if He might delay another hundred years. Maintaining the proper tension between these two attitudes is key for the church's spiritual health. It is not yet time to withdraw from the world and wait for Jesus somewhere in the jungle or in the mountains because Jesus' intercessory prayer for the disciples is still valid today (John 17:15–18). We are in the world with a mission to fulfill. At the same time, without a real sense of Jesus' soon return, the only true motivation for mission disappears and the missionary focus is lost, causing the church to become nothing more than a social club with religious overtones. The sad result is a mission that devolves into preoccupation with results and numbers.

Being ready for Jesus' return involves a daily investment in the advancement of God's kingdom, without pressure for results, greed for gain, or posturing for political advantage. Genuine growth comes from God, not from human methods or efforts (1 Corinthians 3:6, 7). An enduring commitment to these sacred legacies will keep the church strong and vital as it actively waits for His return.

---

1. Robert R. Mathisen, *Critical Issues in American Religious History*, 2nd ed. (Waco, TX: Baylor University Press, 2006), 217.

2. Based on George R. Knight, *Organizing for Mission and Growth: The Development of Adventist Church Structure* (Hagerstown, MD: Review and Herald®, 2006).

3. C. K. Barrett, *A Critical and Exegetical Commentary on the Acts of the Apostles*, vol. 1 (Edinburgh: T&T Clark, 1994), 168.

4. See Darrell L. Bock, *Acts*, Baker Exegetical Commentary on the New Testament (Grand Rapids, MI: Baker Academic, 2007), 149.

5. According to F. F. Bruce, the term *episynagogē* in Hebrews 10:25 for Christian religious meetings suggests that Jewish believers in Jesus "had not yet severed their connection with the synagogue in which they had been brought up," though they could also have special meetings of their own in a more distinct Christian environment. *The Epistle to the Hebrews*, rev. ed. (Grand Rapids, MI: Wm. B. Eerdmans, 1990), 258.

CHAPTER 4

The First Church Leaders

Acts 6:1-8:40

The word of God continued to spread; the number of the disciples increased greatly in Jerusalem, and a great many of the priests became obedient to the faith.

—Acts 6:7, NRSV

When the children of Israel left Egypt, they were an unorganized horde of former slaves. As their leader, Moses faced the overwhelming task of dealing with administrative issues, enacting laws, solving problems, answering questions, and settling disputes. An observation from Jethro, his father-in-law, caused him to realize that he would self-destruct if he did not soon share the burden of leadership. Following Jethro's suggestion, Moses appointed mature men to serve as judges. This shared authority made decision making more efficient, and the people were satisfied.

The plan was twofold: Moses would continue to teach the people God's laws and decide the hard cases, but much of the work would be delegated to capable, respected subordinates who feared God. Following Jethro's advice, he appointed elders from Israel as leaders over groups of one thousand, one hundred, fifty, and ten (Exodus 18:13–27).

Similarly, there came a moment in the life of the infant church when the burdens of leadership became too much for a few men. The fast-growing church in Jerusalem became restless as the leadership struggled to cope with burgeoning responsibilities. It was time to share the load and improve support of the believers. To this end, the appointment of the Seven, as they are called by Luke (Acts 21:8; cf. 6:3), was the first division of ministry that went beyond the apostles to meet the needs of individual congregations. Their selection, it turns out, enhanced the church's world mission. They stepped up to fulfill the commission of Acts 1:8, becoming the first Christian missionaries to preach the gospel beyond Jewish borders (Acts 8:1, 4–8, 26–40; 11:19–21).

Ministering tables

Most converts at Pentecost were Jews from the Greco-Roman world—Hellenistic Jews who were now living in Jerusalem (Acts 2:5, 9–11). Despite being Jews, they were in many respects different from the Palestinian Hebrews mentioned in Acts 6:1. Most notably, they were not acquainted with Aramaic, the language then spoken in Palestine. Due to the language barrier, and in conformity with the usual distribution of Jerusalem's population in different sections of the city, the Hellenists may have also lived together in their own quarter or district where they had their Greek-speaking synagogues (cf. Acts 6:9; 9:29) and guesthouses for pilgrims and fellow visitors.

Yet there were several other differences, both cultural and religious. Having been born in foreign countries, Hellenistic Jews had shallow roots in Palestinian Jewish traditions. They were not as attached to temple ceremonies and aspects of Mosaic law that pertained only to the land of Israel. Additionally, their Greco-Roman background meant they were naturally less fond of Jewish exclusivism and more lenient toward cultural and racial differences. In Palestine, for example, intermarriage between Jews and unconverted Gentiles was strongly prohibited, while elsewhere it tended to be tolerated, as in the case of Timothy's mother (cf. Acts 16:1–3). Because of this, Hellenistic Jews were more open to the inclusive character of the Christian faith. Eventually, it was the influence of Hellenistic believers that moved the church away from outdated rituals and ceremonies to a recognition of their fulfillment in Jesus' life and death.

The differences, mainly religious, between Hellenistic and Palestinian Jews sometimes generated tensions between the groups. From the time of the Maccabees in the second century B.C., there was a tendency to consider those who embraced Greek customs as careless in their observance of the Law (cf. 1 Maccabees 1:10–15; 2 Maccabees 4:7–20). Even if this was not the case in Acts 6, if the apostles neglected people in their busy schedules, chances are they were Hellenists. This contributed to the growing concern that such believers were being adversely affected. Even some of the widows, perhaps living in more peripheral areas, were not receiving proper care (verse 1). The problem is often thought to be the daily distribution of food, supposedly implied in Acts 2:45 and 4:35, but neither the word *food* nor the word *distribution* actually appears in the Greek text of Acts 6:1. The Greek simply reads *diakonia*, "daily ministration." The more likely issue in Acts 2:45 and 4:35 is money, not food.

The solution proposed by the apostles in Acts 6:2, 3 was that the Hellenists choose seven men from among themselves to "minister [*diakoneō*] tables" (verse 2).[1] The apostles would continue to focus their time in prayer and the "ministry [*diakonia*] of the word" (verse 4). Since *diakoneō* and *diakonia* belong to the same word group, the only real difference is between "tables" in verse 2 and "the word" in verse 4. That is, the Seven were supposed to minister "tables," while the Twelve would continue to minister "the word." This, together with the adjective "daily" (verse 1), seems to point to the two main elements of the early church's daily life mentioned in Acts 2:42 and discussed in the previous chapter: teaching ("the word") and fellowship ("tables"), with the latter consisting of the communal meal, the Lord's Supper, and prayers (Acts 2:46; 5:42).

In other words, as the authoritative trustees of Jesus' teachings, the apostles would occupy themselves with the believers' doctrinal instruction while the Seven would be in charge of the fellowship activities in the home churches of Jerusalem and the surrounding area. But their duties were not limited to the responsibilities of deacons as the term is understood today. They were, in fact, the first congregation leaders of the church, and their appointment "provided for eldership as well as the diaconate."[2]

The First Church Leaders

It is unlikely that these two levels of church leadership existed from the very beginning. Chronologically speaking, the first reference to the office of elders in the New Testament comes from the time of Paul's first missionary journey (Acts 14:23), which was some twelve years after the episode of Acts 6,[3] and the first reference to the office of deacons dates from the time of Paul's first imprisonment in Rome (Philippians 1:1), almost thirty years after the appointment of the Seven. In each case, both offices seem to have been in existence for some time.

The Hellenists' witnessing[4]

The activity of the Seven was not restricted to home churches and established believers. They were also engaged in dynamic witnessing, particularly among the Hellenistic Jews of Jerusalem (Acts 6:9, 10). Their efforts were confirmed by several signs and wonders, a number of conversions (verse 7), and strong opposition (verses 11–15). It was in this context that the Seven's activities, particularly Stephen's, drew the church's first systematic persecution (Acts 8:1). This oppression was aimed mainly at the Hellenists, and the apostles and the other Palestinian believers apparently remained untouched (cf. Acts 8:1; 9:30). Forced to leave Jerusalem because of the atrocities perpetrated by the unconverted Paul (Saul) and his band (Acts 8:3; 9:13, 14; 22:4, 5; 26:9–11), those Hellenistic believers became the first Christians to share the gospel with the Samaritans and the Gentiles (Acts 8:4–8; 11:19–21).

But what was it about their successful witness that drew such ferocious persecution? No doubt the central issue in the controversy between the Jews and the Christians was Jesus Christ (cf. Acts 4:1–3, 18; 5:28). Not only did He appear on the Jewish religious scene without going through the conventional qualifying process (John 7:15, 48), He also lacked the credentials of the stereotypical messiah (Matthew 12:38; 13:54–56). Moreover, Jesus' teachings and actions represented a threat to the religious establishment of the day. And above all was the fact that He died on a cross, thus coming under God's curse (Deuteronomy 21:23; cf. Galatians 3:13), disallowing

His claim to be God's Chosen One (cf. 1 Corinthians 1:23).

From the Jewish perspective, the case of the Hellenists was compounded by their criticism of the Levitical ceremonial system. Though Luke offers no detailed account of the Hellenists' understanding of the gospel, the charges raised against Stephen indicate a theological discernment that surpassed that of the Palestinian believers. He was accused of speaking blasphemies against Moses and God (Acts 6:11), that is, against the Law and the temple. Even if he was misunderstood at some points, the charges were accurate. Exhibit A is his explicit condemnation at the Sanhedrin council of the idolatrous veneration of the temple that prevailed in Judaism (Acts 7:48).

In other words, while many Jewish believers of Palestinian origin were finding it difficult to abandon the temple and other ceremonial practices, Stephen, and probably the other Hellenistic believers, understood that Jesus' death signified the end of the entire temple order (Hebrews 8:7, 13; 10:1, 2). It is significant that the only biblical reference to the conversion of priests appears in the context of Stephen's preaching (Acts 6:7).

The same protest against idolizing the temple had been made by Old Testament prophets (Jeremiah 7:4, 10), yet now the situation was different in that it was not only Jewish religiousness that was being called into question but the entire religious system based on the temple and its ceremonies. To the Jewish leaders, this was heresy, blasphemy, and a frontal assault on that which was most sacred in Judaism.

What makes this moment in the church's development important is the prophetic role of Stephen at his trial. His speech before the Sanhedrin (Acts 7:2–53) is the lengthiest one in Acts; and though it seems nothing more than a tedious recital of Israel's history, it echoes the Old Testament covenant and the prophets' call to a backslidden Israel. In these appeals, they sometimes employed the Hebrew word *rîḇ*, which is probably best translated as "covenant lawsuit," to express the idea of God moving a legal action against His people because of their failure to keep the covenant. In Micah 6:1, 2, for example, *rîḇ* occurs three times. Then following the pattern of the Sinai covenant

Stephen and the prophecy of Daniel 9:24-27

Stephen's death is often presented as the event that marks the end of the seventy-week prophecy of Daniel 9:24–27, and there are some reasons for that. One of the six infinitival phrases that summarize what would happen at the end of the prophetic period is "to seal [*hatam*] both vision and prophet" (verse 24, ESV). In addition to "seal up or validate," *hatam* can also mean "to bring to an end," which is preferred here for at least three reasons: (1) this is the meaning of the verb three phrases earlier in the same verse ("to put an end to sin"); (2) it is required by the noun "prophet," which, for being anarthrous, seems to have a corporate meaning; (3) it fits the immediate context better because the seventy weeks were decreed for Daniel's people and his holy city.

This means that "vision" and "prophet" would come to an end by the time this prophetic period closes, and since this period extends half a prophetic week (three and one-half years) beyond the death of the Messiah (verses 26, 27), Stephen's death (A.D. 34) seems to fulfill the requisites for that. The evidences are the *rîb* background and the judgment context of his speech, the lack of any call to repentance, Stephen's break of solidarity with the Jewish leaders, his vision of Jesus in the heavenly court, and the universalization of the gospel after his death.

In this sense, Stephen was the last true prophet to speak particularly to Israel as God's theocratic nation. From then on, God's religion would no longer be centered on Jerusalem, the temple, and its rituals. National Israel would no longer play a role in the conversion of the world.

(Exodus 20–23), Micah reminds the people of God's mighty acts on their behalf (Micah 6:3–5), the stipulations and violations of the covenant (verses 6–12), and, finally, the curses for the violations (verses 13–16).

This is probably the background of Stephen's speech. When

asked to explain his actions, he made no effort to refute the charges or defend his faith. Instead, he raised his voice in the same way the ancient prophets did when they brought God's *rîb* against Israel. His long review of God's past relationship with Israel was intended to emphasize their ingratitude and disobedience. Just before his voice was silenced forever, he was able to bring God's final verdict against them (Acts 7:51–53).

This killing of the Messiah by those Jewish leaders identified them with their "fathers" and filled up the measure of their iniquities. If their fathers were guilty of slaying the prophets, they were even more so for murdering Jesus. The change from "our fathers" (verses 11, 38, 44, 45, NKJV) to "your fathers" (verse 51, NKJV) is significant: Stephen broke his solidarity with his people and took a definite stand for Jesus, the Righteous One (verse 52).

The judgment context of Stephen's speech continues through his vision, which combines two prophetic elements—the Messiah's exaltation (Psalm 110:1) and the heavenly court scene of Daniel 7:9–14 (cf. "the Son of man"). That he saw Jesus standing in the heavenly court (cf. Luke 22:69) seems to mean that the judgment on earth was but an expression of the real judgment in heaven. Like the familiar practice of ancient Near Eastern kings, God rises to pronounce His judgment (Isaiah 3:13; Daniel 12:1).

Unfortunately, this shining moment was the end of Stephen's brief ministry. In an attitude of stubborn defiance that authenticated God's judgment on them, the Jewish leaders once again emulated their fathers (Acts 7:52). They rushed on Stephen, threw him out of the city, and stoned him to death (verses 57–59), thus sealing their fate in God's sovereign plan.

Perhaps this is why the call to repentance, a common feature in the apostles' previous proclamations in Acts (Acts 2:38; 3:19; 5:31), is missing from Stephen's speech. As a prophetic attorney, Stephen brought God's final *rîb* against His people. With the end of Israel's theocracy, the world's salvation would no longer be mediated through national Israel as promised to Abraham (Genesis 12:3; 18:18; 22:18). It would be mediated through the followers of Jesus who, empowered by the Spirit, were now expected to leave Jerusalem and go out to the world.

Concluding remarks

After Stephen's death, the opposition against Hellenistic believers rose to new levels of cruelty, beginning with a massive persecution authorized by the Sanhedrin (Acts 8:1). Instead of silencing their voices, however, the persecution only contributed to spread of the gospel. As New Testament scholar Martin Hengel declares, the Hellenists "became the real founders of the mission to the Gentiles, in which circumcision and the observation of the ritual law were no longer required."[5]

Their legacy, however, went far beyond this. The story of Christian mission did not end with them. In fact, it had only just begun. In the midst of the ensuing persecution, no one less than the chief persecutor, who himself was a Hellenistic Jew (Acts 21:39), was reached by Jesus Christ to become "the ablest defender and most successful herald of the gospel."[6] Stephen's most bitter opponent and the man responsible for his death would carry on with unmatched commitment to the work he had initiated. The power of the gospel, through Hellenists like Paul, changed Christianity forever.

---

1. All Bible quotations in this paragraph are the author's translation.

2. Edmund P. Clowney, *The Church* (Downers Grove, IL: InterVarsity Press, 1995), 213.

3. The reference to elders in Acts 11:30 is controversial, as the episode mentioned there (the so-called famine-relief visit) may have occurred after Paul's first missionary journey, described in chapters 13 and 14. Note that the whole passage (Acts 11:27–30) entails three different chronological levels: the time of the prophecy, which seems to have been prior to Claudius's reign (A.D. 41–54); the time of the famine, which happened in the days of Claudius; and the time of the relief, which supposedly took place at the time of the famine, not at the time of the prophecy. It is not impossible, therefore, that the visit of Acts 11:30 was the same as that of chapter 15 (the Jerusalem council).

4. For most of what follows, see Wilson Paroschi, "The Prophetic Significance of Stephen," *Journal of the Adventist Theological Society* 9, no. 1 (1998): 349–352.

5. Martin Hengel, *Between Jesus and Paul: Studies in the Earliest History of Christianity*, trans. John Bowden (Philadelphia: Fortress Press, 1983), 13.

6. Ellen White, *Sketches From the Life of Paul* (Battle Creek, MI: Review and Herald®, 1883), 9.

CHAPTER 5

The Conversion of Paul

Acts 9:1-30

"Go! This man is my chosen instrument to proclaim my name to the Gentiles and their kings and before the people of Israel."
—Acts 9:15, NIV

Conversion on the Way to Damascus, painted by Caravaggio in 1601, is a masterpiece of Italian Renaissance art. Using shadow and light to focus the viewer's attention on key areas, the painting illustrates the moment of Saul's conversion, when Jesus Christ Himself appears to him saying, "Saul, Saul, why are you persecuting me?" (Acts 9:4, ESV). Intense and stripped of all distraction, there is Saul in the forefront, in a position that simulates a 3-D effect. In the center, his horse and a groom seem unaware of his mighty struggle. With his whole world turned upside down, he remains motionless on the ground, shattered and humbled. There is no sign of his former power and dignity save the helmet, sword, and cloak next to him. Blinded by the divine light, he stretches his arms into the air, hands splayed as if desperately searching for answers.

The extraordinary painting mirrors the biblical narrative. Caravaggio was able to capture the import of Saul's encounter with Jesus near Damascus, which was undoubtedly the most critical moment the young Pharisee had ever experienced. At that moment, God was intervening in his life to give him a chance to confront his errors and change his course. And Saul did. He faithfully responded to God's call to become the apostle who universalized the gospel, both geographically and theologically.

The Conversion of Paul

The pre-Christian Paul

The New Testament contains precious background information that helps us understand this gospel herald. Here are the most significant facts:

1. *Born in Tarsus of Cilicia.* Paul was a Hellenistic Jew. His birthplace was Tarsus, the capital of the Roman province of Cilicia, located in the southeastern part of Asia Minor (modern Turkey). Judging from its remains, first-century Tarsus must have housed a population of no less than half a million people, making it one of the most important cities of the Mediterranean world. As a dynamic center of Hellenistic culture, its schools of philosophy and rhetoric are said to have surpassed those of Athens and Alexandria. Such a rich cultural environment certainly influenced Paul in his early years. It was in Tarsus he learned Greek, and probably Latin.

2. *Roman citizen.* Unlike many other Jews of his day, Paul was a Roman citizen by birth (Acts 22:28), which means his father must have been a Roman citizen before him. Originally restricted to freeborn natives of Rome, this particular era allowed the purchase of Roman citizenship or conferral on select provincial subjects who had performed exceptional services for the Roman cause. How Paul's family of origin attained citizenship is unknown, but any Roman citizen benefited from numerous rights and privileges, such as exemption from some taxes, a fair public trial, the right to appeal to the emperor, immunity against some forms of punishments, and, in case of the death penalty, protection against crucifixion. Paul knew his rights and used them wisely (Acts 16:35–39; 22:25–29; 25:10–12).

3. *Pure-blood Jew.* In Jewish tradition, a Jew is any person born to a Jewish mother. This was, for example, Timothy's case (Acts 16:1–3). Any Gentile converted to Judaism through circumcision—called a proselyte (cf. Acts 2:11; 6:5; 13:43)—was also considered a Jew. Paul, however, was neither the son of a mixed marriage nor a converted Gentile. In Philippians 3:5, he says he was "of the people of Israel" and a "Hebrew of Hebrews," meaning he was born of pure Hebrew stock.

Additionally, he was "of the tribe of Benjamin," the sole tribe remaining loyal to Judah when the northern kingdom broke away (1 Kings 12:21–23). His Jewishness, therefore, was beyond dispute and traceable to Abraham himself (cf. Romans 11:1; 2 Corinthians 11:22).

4. *Faithful to Jewish tradition.* Despite living in the Greco-Roman world, Paul's family did not neglect their Jewish duties. Paul was "circumcised on the eighth day" (Philippians 3:5, NIV), exactly according to the Law (Leviticus 12:3). From the cradle, he was nursed in the ancestral faith as he grew and matured. As a youth, he was far ahead of his peers in zeal for the fathers' traditions (Galatians 1:14; Acts 22:3), to the point of being blameless concerning religious aspects that could be observed by human eyes (Philippians 3:6).

5. *Grew up in Jerusalem.* While still a child, Paul's family moved to Jerusalem, where he was educated under Gamaliel (Acts 22:3; cf. Acts 23:16), a well-known and celebrated rabbi. His instruction would have finished around the age of eighteen or twenty, when a Jewish lad was expected to marry. Since evidence that Paul met Jesus before his conversion is lacking, it is tempting to say he completed his rabbinic studies just before Jesus started His public ministry, possibly returning to Tarsus to improve his secular education during this time period.[1] There were great educational resources in Tarsus, and since Acts and Paul's own letters suggest he was learned in rhetoric, philosophy, and Roman law, the Tarsus theory is plausible. A few years later, perhaps just before Stephen's appointment (cf. Acts 7:58), he would have returned to Jerusalem to pursue his own rabbinic career.

6. *Pharisee.* Like Gamaliel, Paul was a Pharisee (Philippians 3:5; cf. Acts 23:6; 26:5). In fact, most rabbis (or scribes) were Pharisees. First-century Judaism was divided into several opposing religious groups, including the Pharisees, the Sadducees, the Zealots, and the Essenes. Pharisees were the largest of these groups and exerted the strongest influence among the common people. Pharisaism's main characteristics were extreme concern for ritual purification and observance of the oral and written

law. For these reasons, Pharisees tended to be condescending to other Jews, legalistic, and hypocritical. But to their credit, many were sincere and tried to live faithfully before God. Paul was one of those (Philippians 3:4–6; cf. Acts 23:1).

7. *Member of the Sanhedrin.* The Sanhedrin at Jerusalem was the highest tribunal of the Jews. It dealt with both religious and civil matters, with the high priest serving as president over seventy members, mostly Sadducees and Pharisees (cf. Acts 23:6). Paul's preconversion vote against the followers of Jesus during the persecution (Acts 26:10; cf. Acts 22:20) implies that, despite his young age, he was a member of the Sanhedrin. He would have been about twenty-five at the time.

8. *Shaliah.* The Jews living outside Palestine were organized in a kind of network with headquarters in Jerusalem (the Sanhedrin), and the outlying synagogues served as support centers for the local communities. There was constant communication between the Sanhedrin and such communities through letters that were normally carried by a *shaliah*, "one who is sent" (from the Hebrew *shalah*, "to send") (cf. Acts 28:21). A *shaliah* was an official agent, designated by the Sanhedrin, to perform several religious functions. When Paul asked the high priest for letters addressed to the synagogues in Damascus (Acts 9:1, 2; 22:5), he became a *shaliah* with the authority to arrest the followers of Jesus and bring them to Jerusalem (cf. Acts 26:12). In Greek, the equivalent to *shaliah* is *apostolos*, the root word for *apostle*. So before being an apostle of Jesus Christ, Paul was an apostle of Judaism.

Conversion near Damascus

There are four New Testament accounts of Paul's conversion and early apostolic activities: three in Acts (Acts 9:1–30; 22:3–21; 26:9–18) and one in Galatians 1:13–24. Allusions to them can also be found elsewhere in Paul's writings (1 Corinthians 9:1; 15:8; 2 Corinthians 11:32, 33; Philippians 3:7–9). The conversion accounts are not identical and do not necessarily provide a full description of what happened. But they complement each and offer important insights on the conversion's impact on Paul's life.

Struck by the divine light, Saul hears a strange and authoritative voice solemnly address him in his mother tongue, "Saul, Saul, why are you persecuting me?" (Acts 9:4, ESV; cf. Acts 22:7). Utterly confused, the only thing he can sense is that he is in the divine presence, so he responds, "Who are you, Lord?" (Acts 9:5, ESV; cf. Acts 22:8). This is the first of two questions that would change his life forever. With dreadful surprise, he hears the unwanted answer, "I am Jesus the Nazarene, whom you are persecuting" (Acts 22:8, NASB).

From the outset, Saul learned three important lessons. First, Jesus identifies with His followers on earth (Romans 12:4, 5; 1 Corinthians 12:27), and any harm done to them is harm done to Himself. Second, Jesus is indeed alive. This means His followers were right about His resurrection and the Jewish authorities were not (Matthew 28:11–15; Acts 4:1–3). And third, Gamaliel's advice to the Sanhedrin was sound: leave the disciples undisturbed because they might end up fighting against God (Acts 5:33–39).[2]

Paul would learn important lessons about the gospel during the next three years of his apostolic apprenticeship.[3] The first such lesson was the meaning of Jesus' death. "From now on, we regard no one according to the flesh. Even though we have known Christ according to the flesh, yet now we know Him thus no longer" (2 Corinthians 5:16, NKJV). This passage has no relevance to the issue of whether or not Paul had known Jesus before his conversion, much less that he had yielded his interest in the earthly, physical Jesus to the risen, spiritual Christ. The contrast being conveyed is between Paul's former and present attitude toward Christ, and to people in general. Since he is now "in Christ" and considers himself "a new creation" (verse 17, NKJV), the apostle's perspective has changed, thus allowing him to see Jesus Christ differently than before. This is why, in several recent translations, the expression "according to the flesh"—the literal Greek rendering—is replaced by "from a human point of view" or an equivalent (cf. NRSV, NIV, NJB, NLT, NEB).

Seneca once said, "I do not trust the eyes, but the mind, to tell me what a man is, and to distinguish what is true from what is false."[4] It is far easier to judge people by outward appearances, and this is how Paul had come to view Jesus as an impostor. The cross not only showed Christ was unmistakably under God's curse (Deuteronomy 21:23), it also posed an insuperable stumbling block (1 Corinthians 1:23). But Paul's experience on the Damascus road forced him to reevaluate his convictions about Jesus, most notably His death. Jesus had died under God's curse—a curse that originally belonged to humankind—and His vicarious death brought deliverance to all (Romans 5:6–8). He became a curse for us to redeem us from the curse of the law (Galatians 3:13, ESV). This is the essence of the gospel.

Second, such understanding of Jesus' death also made Paul reconsider his opinion of himself. Judaism did not believe in hereditary corruption and depravity. Sin was a matter of choice and occurred when a person wandered and deliberately refused to obey God's will (cf. Acts 25:8). If a choice got you into sin, a choice could get you out, thus making justification by works possible (Romans 10:3). As a Pharisee, Paul looked at his own spiritual accomplishments with pride and satisfaction (Philippians 3:6); but after his conversion, he came to a more realistic understanding of human nature (Romans 7:14, 17, 20). He came to the conviction that it was impossible for humans to attain righteousness before God (Romans 3:19, 20; 9:31, 32; Galatians 3:10, 11; 5:2–4). Everything he once thought to be valuable in this sense, he came to consider worthless because of Christ. His only wish was to be found in Him, not having a righteousness of his own but a righteousness through faith (Philippians 3:7–9).

And finally, Paul's conversion led him to reassess the Gentiles' place in salvation history. When he understood that Jesus "died for all" (2 Corinthians 5:14, 15, NKJV), whether Jew or non-Jew, he no longer saw the latter "from a human point of view" (verse 16, NLT). He understood that the traditional Jewish standards were faulty because they rested on external criteria, such as human descent, covenant membership, circumcision,

Stephen and Paul's conversion

According to Acts 26:14, when Jesus first addressed Saul near Damascus, He added this proverbial saying: "It is hard for you to kick against the goads" (ESV). The sense of this idiom is that it is foolish to struggle against one's destiny. This saying may point to Saul's uneasy conscience, possibly harkening to his debates with Stephen.

Even with all his theological training, Saul was not able to refute Stephen's presentation of the gospel (Acts 6:10). By praying for his executioners (Acts 7:60), Stephen surely left a disturbing impression on Saul's mind, but still Saul resisted. Jesus was trying to reach out and include him in His plans, and he continued fighting until he realized that he was on the wrong side (Acts 26:9). As Augustine said, "If Stephen had not prayed . . . , the church would not have Paul."[5]

and observance of the law (Romans 4:18; 9:7; Galatians 3:6–9, 13, 14). No longer did he think Gentiles could not be saved without first converting to Judaism (Acts 15:1, 5) or relegate them to second-class citizenship in God's kingdom.

Knowing there is only one God, Paul came to realize there can be only one gospel—the gospel of salvation by faith alone, for both Jews and Gentiles alike (Romans 3:29, 30; 9:30–32; 10:12, 13). This radical shift caused him to abandon old stereotypes and declare that "there is neither Jew nor Greek, there is neither slave nor free, there is no male and female, for you are all one in Christ Jesus" (Galatians 3:28, ESV).

With his second question on the Damascus road, "What shall I do, Lord?" (Acts 22:10, ESV), he set the course for the rest of his life. After sensing the voice belonged to Jesus, he was overwhelmed with conviction and committed his life to God. He had always been zealous in His service, and it would be no different now. God had chosen him to bear witness "to the Gentiles and their kings and to the people of Israel"

(Acts 9:15, NIV). He surrendered himself to his new destiny, regained his sight, and with new humility, began to see things as they really were and not merely "from a human point of view."

Concluding remarks

Paul's conversion was the most remarkable event in the post-Pentecost church. God knew the harm he could do to the infant church and decided to be intentional toward him (Galatians 1:15). If he could win Saul to His side, not only would persecution wane but the gospel cause would be significantly strengthened. Fortunately, Paul "was not disobedient to the heavenly vision" (Acts 26:19, ESV) and made a tremendous impact for the gospel.

While it is true that his persecuting past would always bring a deep sense of unworthiness, he could say with a still deeper sense of gratitude that God's grace to him had not been in vain. He would always think of himself as the least of the apostles yet honestly admitted to working harder than any of them (1 Corinthians 15:9, 10). Today, his legacy in apostolic history is unsurpassed.

----

1. That Paul had strong connections with Tarsus and not only vague memories from childhood seems implied from at least one episode. When the Hellenistic Jews of Jerusalem started planning his death during his first visit to the city after his conversion, he went to Tarsus (Acts 9:26–30; 22:17–21), where he seems to have stayed for about six years (c. A.D. 38–44). During this time, he worked with both Jews and Gentiles (cf. Acts 22:21) and established Christianity in Cilicia (cf. Acts 15:40, 41).

2. See David J. Williams, *Acts* (Grand Rapids, MI: Baker Books, 1990), 169.

3. See Ellen White, *The Acts of the Apostles* (Mountain View, CA: Pacific Press®, 1911), 125.

4. Seneca, *De vita beata* 2.2.

5. Augustine, "*Sermo 382: Sermo In Natale Sancti Stephani Primi Martiris,*" *Sant Agostino: Sermones S. Augustini Opera Omnia,* http://www.augustinus.it/latino /discorsi/index2.htm, translated by the author

CHAPTER 6

The Ministry of Peter

Acts 9:31-12:25

Then Peter began to speak to them: "I truly understand that God shows no partiality, but in every nation anyone who fears him and does what is right is acceptable to him."

—Acts 10:34, 35, NRSV

Ancient Greeks divided humanity into two groups: themselves and the barbarians. The latter group consisted of everyone who did not speak Greek. The term *barbaros* is onomatopoeic; that is, it represents a phonetic attempt to reproduce the sound it describes. To Greek ears, foreign languages sounded so much like babbling that they were imitated by saying, "Bar, bar, bar." Later, *barbaros* acquired a derogatory nuance, being used as a synonym for wild, cruel, and uncivilized behavior (cf. 2 Maccabees 4:25; 10:4). In Romans 1:14, for example, Paul acknowledges a debt to both Greeks and barbarians, who are then contrasted with the wise and the foolish.

The Jews also divided humanity into two groups: themselves and the Gentiles, with the latter being everyone who was not Jewish. And as with the Greeks, they also ended up distinguishing themselves from other people groups in a narrow, exclusive sense. So much so that by the time of Jesus the Jews had developed a hard and discriminatory attitude to foreigners, and "Gentile" had become a label of scorn equal in shame to "tax-collector" (Matthew 18:17, NRSV).

This posed enormous difficulties for a church that was supposed to extend its evangelistic efforts to the ends of the earth, far beyond Jewish confines. In fact, since it had the potential for dividing the church and neutralizing the gospel message, this cultural attitude became a serious issue for the early believers.

In its infancy, the church enjoyed relative peace throughout Palestine after the conversion of Paul (Acts 9:31), with the apostles going from place to place strengthening the believers (verses 32–43). At the same time, God would use Peter, the most influential among the Twelve, to break the church's resistance against Gentile conversion (Acts 10:1–11:18). This development marked the beginning of a long battle that would consume much of Paul's time and energy.

Jews and Gentiles

The term *Gentile* comes from Latin; and in the plural, it renders the Greek *ta ethnē* used both in the New Testament and the Greek Old Testament (the Septuagint) for "nations, foreigners, or heathen." In the Hebrew Old Testament, the term is *gôyim* (singular, *gôy*), which bears similar meaning.

In God's covenant with Abraham, his descendants are distinguished from other peoples but not in any restricted sense (cf. Genesis 12:2; 18:18; 22:18; 26:4). It was after the Exodus and the Sinai covenant that Israel became conscious of its distinctiveness from other nations by being separated to God (Exodus 19:6; Deuteronomy 26:5; cf. Genesis 12:1, 2). From then on, this consciousness was to guide the Israelites in their relations with other peoples (Exodus 34:10; Deuteronomy 15:6). They were to remain consecrated to God and shun the contaminations of those around them (Exodus 34:12–16; Leviticus 18:24–27; Deuteronomy 7:3–5).

This charter, however, did not diminish the temptation to compromise with the surrounding idolatry and immorality (2 Kings 14:24). Israel's weakness in this regard brought God's judgment on Israel (2 Kings 17:7–18) and then on Judah as well (Ezekiel 5:5–17). Upon their return from the Babylonian exile, the danger continued (Ezra 4:1–5; 9:1–3) and was more insidious because of the corrupt Jews who had remained in the land (cf. Ezra 6:21). It was in this context that Ezra and Nehemiah promoted significant reforms aimed at strengthening

Jewish identity as a strictly religious community.

To achieve this, they decided to eliminate most opportunities for idolatry by cleansing the congregation of all pagan elements, calling for a public confession of sin and restoration of the temple services (Ezra 10:1–4, 10–12, 16, 17; Nehemiah 9:1–3; 13:1–30; cf. Malachi 2:11–16). And it worked. No matter their faults in later periods, the Jews were virtually healed of idolatry. They never returned to the idolatrous practices of the nations around them to this degree.

Yet the fact that they did not have political freedom, except for a brief time under the Hasmoneans (142–63 B.C.), made it nearly impossible to prevent the advance of pagan culture in their midst. Many Gentiles lived in Palestine, and they even outnumbered the Jewish population in several places. In this situation, the average Jew would likely be in daily contact with pagan affairs, if not with the people themselves, at least with the commodities and objects that were brought to Palestine by way of trade and commerce. The very silver coins in circulation bore the emperor's image and were indispensable pagan elements in daily Jewish life (cf. Matthew 22:19–21).

All of this, not to mention the cruel treatment they suffered at the hand of foreign oppressors such as the Seleucids and eventually the Romans, caused the Jews to develop an increasing hostility toward Gentiles. Over time, their constant exposure to paganism made them less sympathetic to Gentiles. In a sense, one can understand why Tacitus, the Roman writer, would say they regarded the rest of humankind with all the hatred of enemies.[1]

In the Old Testament, provision had been made for foreigners who wished to live in Israel, so-called resident aliens. The Hebrew term generally used for such people is *gērim* (singular, *gēr*). The Old Testament repeatedly emphasizes the obligation to welcome such people (Deuteronomy 10:17–19), who were mostly laborers and artisans. Joining Israelite society meant following Israelite laws (Leviticus 24:22; Numbers 15:15, 16), though not necessarily the ceremonial laws. That is, it was not mandatory to adopt the Israelite religion.

Essential to this process, of course, was the renunciation of paganism—along with the various forms of immorality (incest, adultery, ritual infanticide, homosexual intercourse) that invariably accompanied it—and the adoption of monotheism (Leviticus 17:1–18:30; 20:2; cf. Ezekiel 14:5–8; Romans 1:18–32). These factors distinguished Hebrews from pagans and stood as absolute conditions, with no room for concessions (cf. Leviticus 18:24–30). Under foreigner occupation, however, the Jews had no authority to enforce such requirements and could do nothing more than tolerate the pagans and the threat they posed to their religion.

This led to the development, probably around the second century B.C., of a concept known as defilement by association. According to this belief, if something clean touched something unclean, it became polluted. Though not intrinsically unclean, Gentiles were functionally unclean due to their enduring attachment to idols and depravity. Additionally, sexual and cultic sins were moral offenses and, as such, the defilement they produced was not contagious. Most Jews, however, would avoid contact with Gentiles for the sake of ritual purity.

In the passage mentioned above, Tacitus condemns the Jews for their exclusivism and refusal to associate with non-Jews; a judgment which is confirmed by several Jewish texts of the era, including Flavius Josephus (Tobit 1:10–12; Judith 12:1–4; Jubilees 22:16; Joseph and Aseneth 7:1; Josephus, *Antiquities of the Jews* 13.8.3; Josephus, *Against Apion* 2.29). Jews, for example, would not enter a Gentile's house, much less eat with him, because this would render them ritually unclean for seven days (cf. Numbers 19:11, 14).[2]

This custom shaped the Jewish leaders' denial to enter Pilate's residence in Jerusalem during the trial of Jesus (John 18:28). Moreover, everything that was purchased from a Gentile needed purification before being used by Jews; some of the most ordinary foods were disallowed because Jewish laws had not been observed in the course of production. Such was the case with bread, oil, and milk, unless the milking had been witnessed by a Jew. This made traveling in Gentile countries highly problematic for orthodox Jews. Even if they ate only raw fruits and vegetables, they would need to undergo ritual purification upon returning home. This is what Paul did in Jerusalem at the end of his third missionary journey, before going to the priests (Acts 21:26; cf. verses 23, 24).

Nevertheless, any Gentile could be converted to Judaism and become a proselyte (from the Greek *prosēlytos*, "convert"). When that happened, the restrictions and hostilities would disappear, and the person would be granted most—but not all—privileges of ethnic Jews (cf. Exodus 12:48). Proselytes, for example, could not be accepted as members of the Sanhedrin, and no priest could ever marry a proselyte woman, unless her mother was Jew; this regulation was valid even to the tenth generation.

While the temple stood, proselytes were required to meet three demands for the acceptance into Judaism: circumcision, baptism (for purification purposes), and an animal sacrifice. In the case of women, only the last two were required. Beyond this, the rabbis' attitudes to converted Gentiles were generally mixed. Most of them were favorably disposed, and some would venture to say that a Gentile "who has become a proselyte is like a child newly born"[3] (cf. John 3:3–5). The few exceptions in which a rabbi's attitude was negative usually indicated the failure of some converts to live up to their commitment.

Cornelius's conversion

Up to the destruction of Jerusalem in A.D. 70, many individuals converted to Judaism. This seems strange in view of the prevailing Greco-Roman hostility toward the Jews. Imageless worship, a peculiar lifestyle (especially Sabbath observance and abstention from pork), and a sense of exclusivity marked the Jews and made them easy targets of indignation and violence. Yet dissatisfaction with pagan religions drove many people to Judaism. Women, in particular, were attracted to the high ethical standards and the belief in the afterlife. Circumcision, however, was a serious obstacle. With their emphasis on aesthetics, ancient Greeks and Romans considered circumcision a mutilation of a perfect form. Consequently, Gentiles would often attach themselves to the synagogue, worshiping there and adopting Jewish religious practices, without becoming proselytes in the full sense of the word. Luke's account refers to these believers as God fearers (Acts 13:16, 26; 16:14) and those who were God worshipers (Acts 13:50; 16:14; 17:4, 17; 18:7). Cornelius was one of them (Acts 10:2, 22).

He lived in Caesarea, a magnificent coastal city seventy miles northwest of Jerusalem. It was the center of the Roman administration in Judea and the main garrison of the provincial troops, of which Cornelius was a centurion (verse 1). He and his household were faithful to God and known among the people by their practical piety (verse 2; cf. verses 4, 22). In a God-given vision, he was instructed by an angel to send messengers to Joppa, some twenty-five miles south, and invite Peter to visit him (verses 5–8).

As the messengers approached Joppa, Peter received a vision. He saw coming down from heaven a large sheet full of clean and unclean animals, followed by a voice commanding him to kill and eat (verses 9–13; cf. Acts 11:5–7). In refusing to obey the command, Peter explained he had never eaten anything "common" (*koinos*) or "unclean" (*akathartos*) (Acts 10:14, ESV; cf. Acts 11:8). The voice replied, "What God has made clean, do not call common [*koinoō*]" (Acts 10:15, ESV; cf. Acts 11:9).

This vision has been traditionally interpreted to mean that Levitical food laws (Leviticus 11:3–43; cf. Deuteronomy 14:3–21) are now obsolete.[4] But a clearer understanding of the passage is gained by carefully noting two key words in the dialogue; *koinos* ("common") and *akathartos* ("unclean"). The word *koinos* ("common") and its verbal cognate *koinoō* ("to render common") are not synonyms for *akathartos* ("unclean"). They represent two different concepts, one biblical and one extrabiblical.

When referring to "unclean" animals, the Greek Old Testament consistently uses *akathartos*, not *koinos*. The use of *koinos* or *koinoō*, as found in Peter's vision for "common, or to render common," has to do with the rabbinic concept of defilement by association of which linguistic evidence can be found in inter-testamental and first-century Jewish literature,[5] where *koinos* is explicitly used of Gentiles.[6]

The Leviticus dietary laws

The distinction between clean and unclean animals detailed in Leviticus 11:3–43 (cf. Deuteronomy 14:3–21) predates the Sinai covenant. It is pre-Mosaic, antediluvian (Genesis 7:2, 8; 8:20), and universally applicable. In addition, the uncleanness of unclean animals is permanent. In the entire Old Testament, there is no mention of any purification rite that can remove the uncleanness of such animals. Also, the uncleanness of unclean (living) animals is not contagious. That is, it cannot defile or pollute clean animals, objects, or persons (cf. Mark 11:7). Leviticus 7:19 refers only to peace offerings.

Finally, the Levitical dietary laws were not linked to any ceremony of the Israelite sanctuary, indicating that their violation did not cause ceremonial defilement or prevent the person from worshiping God. They were also not typo-logical in nature, meaning they cannot be equated with those ritual laws that were abolished by Jesus' death on the cross. Eating unclean meat is a moral sin equivalent to idolatry and immorality (Isaiah 65:2–7; 66:17; Ezekiel 33:25, 26) and violates God's permanent call to holiness (Leviticus 11:44, 45; cf. 1 Peter 1:16).

This was the issue in Peter's vision. What troubled him with the command to "kill and eat" (Acts 10:13, ESV) was not the idea of consuming unclean food but, rather, the scandal of eat-ing clean food that had supposedly been defiled—made com-mon or profane (cf. NABRE, NJB)—through contact with the unclean. It is worth noting that, though Peter spoke of the "common or unclean," the heavenly voice itself referred only to the first of these two terms, thus rebuking the apostle for assuming that animals created clean by God could have been defiled by association with unclean ones. And in Acts 10:28, Peter shows that this was the real purpose of the vision; not to do away with the Levitical food laws but to end his—and by extension the early church's—prejudice against Gentiles. As a law-abiding Jew, Peter believed that if he entered Cornelius's house, he would instantly contract ceremonial defilement and so become unfit to join in the worship of God. Irrespective of the food motif and Peter's immediate feelings, the vision was given to convince him that "God shows no partiality, but in every nation anyone who fears him and does what is right is acceptable to him" (verses 34, 35, ESV).

It should be stressed that this idea is also present in the Old Testament. God had always intended Gentiles to share in the blessings of Abraham (Genesis 12:3; 17:4, 5). According to the prophets, Gentiles would be assigned a place in the Messianic kingdom (Isaiah 60:5, 6). They would seek the Lord, and the Messiah would be a light to them (Isaiah 42:6), bringing salvation to the ends of the earth (Isaiah 49:6).

Concluding remarks

When Peter was sharing the gospel with Cornelius and his family (Acts 10:36–43), the Holy Spirit, with Pentecost power, assured the apostle and his companions about the vision (verses 45–48). The gift of tongues at Cornelius's home apparently had no other purpose than to show its legitimacy in the life of the church. No other manifestation of tongues in connection with conversion is recorded in the New Testament, and later, when censured by the Jerusalem believers for eating in a Gentile's house (Acts 11:1–3), Peter cited both the vision (verses 4–14) and the tongues phenomenon (verses 15–17) as justification for his actions. His detractors fell silent and subsequently acknowledged that the Gentiles had also been given repentance for salvation (verse 18).

Nevertheless, it seems this discussion centered on the issue of ceremonial purity rather than on the necessity of circumcision for salvation. Of course, circumcision continued to vex the early church. A few years later, during the Jerusalem Council, it would be important to recall that God had used Peter, not the unknown and suspicious Paul, to bring the first uncircumcised Gentiles to faith (Acts 15:7–11). Though the problem lingered, as evidenced by Paul's remarks in Romans and Galatians, Peter's experience with Cornelius was a watershed moment in the history of the early church.

Meanwhile in Syrian Antioch, Gentiles were joining the faith, thanks to the missionary efforts of the Hellenistic refugees from Jerusalem (Acts 11:19–21). It was in this context that Paul's independent work in Cilicia would come to an end (cf. Acts 9:30), and he would make Antioch the new center of his apostolic ministry (Acts 11:25, 26; 13:1–3; 14:26–28; 15:22–35; 18:22). In spite of the early Palestinian believers' ongoing struggle with ceremonial purity, the expected universalization of the faith (Acts 1:8) was already taking off successfully.

---

1. Tacitus, *The Histories* 5.5.

2. The seven-day rule, which was connected with dead corpses (Numbers 19:11, 14; cf. Numbers 9:6–10), applied in this case because the Gentiles were thought to throw abortions down their drains. *The Mishnah*, trans. Herbert Danby (Oxford: Oxford University Press, 1933), 675n10.

3. Babylonian Talmud: Yebamoth 48b.

4. E.g., "Clearly, it had to do with the cancellation of the Jewish dietary laws." David J. Williams, *Acts* (Grand Rapids, MI: Baker Books, 1990), 188.

5. For example, 1 Maccabees 1:47, Josephus, *The Antiquities of the Jews* 3.7.7; 11.5.7; 12.8.5; 13.1.1; cf. *Letter of Aristeas* 315, where *koinos* is explicitly used of Gentiles.

6. See esp. Colin House, "Defilement by Association: Some Insights From the Usage of *koinos/koinnoō* in Acts 10 and 11," *Andrews University Seminary Studies* 21, no. 2 (Summer 1983): 143–153.

CHAPTER 7

Paul's First
Missionary Journey

Acts 13:1-14:28

*"Therefore, my friends, I want you to know that through Jesus
the forgiveness of sins is proclaimed to you. Through him
everyone who believes is set free from every sin, a justification you
were not able to obtain under the law of Moses."*
—Acts 13:38, 39, NIV

The Angrogna Valley, located in the Alpine region of Pied-
mont, Italy, is one of four major valleys that form the historic
home of the Waldenses. Remembered for their dedication and
perseverance, these believers' unfailing loyalty to Scripture in
the face of ruthless persecution continues to inspire. At the far
end of the valley lies Pra del Torno, the most isolated hamlet in
the rocky heights of Angrogna. Until the mid-twentieth century, narrow gorges allowed for only a mule track to the bottom of the valley.

This isolation is what caused the Waldenses to choose Pra
del Torno for their final resistance and refuge during the persecution of the Savoy government. For this same reason, Pra
del Torno was the training place for the *barba*, the Waldensian
pastors and missionaries. On the upper end of the hamlet,
there still stands a rustic stone building where it is believed the
Collegio dei Barba once existed, between the fourteenth and
sixteenth centuries.

Stepping inside the old structure, squinting in the small
room's dim light, it is possible to imagine the *barba* studying
around the large stone table. A Bible, their only textbook, still lies
open as a testament to their faith and commitment. From this
place, after three or four years of study, students emerged during

61

the winter season. After a consecration, they would embark on their dangerous journey, usually two by two. Their mission would often last the rest of their lives—until they were exhausted or martyred. In so doing, they followed in the footsteps of Paul, embracing the same mission he had received from Christ.[1]

Acts records Paul's three missionary journeys to the Gentiles. The first one (Acts 13; 14) was the shortest, both in time and distance. Yet this journey marked his official debut as a missionary to the Gentiles and, in particular, caused the church to address the Gentile problem more thoroughly than in the case of Cornelius. This proved to be the greatest challenge Paul faced in his entire ministry.

The gospel in Antioch

Although receiving his apostleship and missionary assignment directly from Jesus Christ, Paul's mission to the Gentiles was inextricably linked to the church in Syrian Antioch, which was the first and most important Christian center outside of Jerusalem. Antioch, some three hundred miles north of Jerusalem, was the capital of the Roman province of Syria and the third largest city in the empire after Rome and Alexandria. Its population of eight hundred thousand was mixed and included a large number of Jews who enjoyed full rights. Josephus praises the beauty of its great synagogue, whose services attracted a multitude of Gentiles who had incorporated themselves into the Jewish community as proselytes.[2] Nicolaus, one of the converts at Pentecost and last in the list of the Seven, was a proselyte from Antioch (Acts 6:5).

The church was established there in the aftermath of the persecution that followed Stephen's death. Luke states that some of the Hellenistic believers from Jerusalem fled north, where they probably set up congregations in Ptolemais, Tyre, and Sidon (Acts 21:3, 4, 7; 27:3). From these city ports, some sailed to Cyprus and some to Antioch in Syria. Because of their preaching to the Jews in Antioch, they began to make inroads with the Gentiles as well. Before long, many of them accepted the faith (Acts 14:21).

By this time, Paul had already been in Tarsus for several years (cf. Acts 9:30), apparently working all by himself among both Jews and Gentiles (cf. Acts 22:21) with some measure of success (cf. Acts 15:41). But there is no further information about this period of ministry, so this report from Antioch is the first we have of Gentiles joining the faith in large scale. This explains why the first cosmopolitan Christian congregation was formed in this city.

News of such developments reached the church leaders in Jerusalem, and Barnabas was sent to investigate (verse 22). Attitudes may not have been hostile at this point, but dramatic change was on the horizon, giving rise to one of the most difficult chapters in the history of the early church.

Barnabas, a Hellenistic Jew from Cyprus, had possible connections with Cypriots who had come to Antioch (Acts 11:20). Whatever his specific assignment was, he noticed opportunities for the advancement of the gospel, so he went to Paul in Tarsus, feeling he could be a vital help (verse 25). Their year together saw large crowds of people, mostly Gentiles, hearing and accepting the gospel. The final stage of Jesus' commission in Acts 1:8 was in full progress. Here in Antioch believers were first called "Christians" (verse 26)—a term not as geographically restricted as "Nazarenes," which was initially used in Jewish circles (cf. Acts 24:5).

With the apostles still positioned in Jerusalem, Syrian Antioch eventually occupied a place of honor in the history of the church, being recognized as the birthplace of Christian missions. The missionary zeal of those who first preached the gospel there was such that it continued to reverberate among the new believers. Ellen White lauds this strength of early Christianity when she states that "every true Christian will possess a missionary spirit."[3]

After a full year of local evangelism, Barnabas and Paul, still under Barnabas's leadership (Acts 13:1, 2, 7), were sent by the church on a missionary journey through foreign lands. In the early part of the journey, they were accompanied by John Mark, Barnabas's cousin. This is the first missionary endeavor in Acts that is intentional and carefully planned, yet Luke makes it clear that God was the one who took the initiative (Acts 13:2). He works through human decisions, but salvation history follows a superior plan—one conceived in the heart and mind of God (cf. Acts 2:23; 4:27, 28; 13:36).

Their first destination was the island of Cyprus, a Roman province in the northeast corner of the Mediterranean Sea and not far from Antioch. Cyprus seemed a natural place to start because not only was Barnabas from there but the local Jewish population was also large enough to support a number of synagogues. These worship centers could be used as forums to preach the gospel to both Jews and Gentiles. Moreover, the gospel had already been introduced on the island through Hellenistic refugees from Jerusalem (Acts 11:19, 20), opening the way for further missionary work.

From Cyprus, Barnabas and Paul sailed northwest to Perga, located in Pamphylia on the south central coast of Asia Minor (modern Turkey). From there, they proceeded, now by land, to Pisidian Antioch, the leading city in Phrygia, then to Iconium, still in Phrygia (Acts 13:51), and finally to Lystra and Derbe, in Lycaonia (Acts 14:6). According to the political divisions of the time, these four cities were part of the province of Galatia, to whom Paul would write one of his main letters some time later. After Derbe, the missionaries retraced their steps to Perga and then to Syrian Antioch (verses 25, 26).

The whole journey seems to have lasted more than two years, but they accomplished a great deal even though they only covered about 1,200 miles (cf. Acts 13:49, 52; 14:1, 3, 6, 7, 21, 25). Mobility was essential to govern the vast empire; and under Roman rule, travel conditions were better than at any other period of human history before the nineteenth century.[4] Most of the empire was at peace, with minimal military activity, the so-called *Pax Romana* (Roman peace). The Mediterranean, which had a long history of piracy and raiding, was a safe place to travel. About fifty-three thousand miles of roads, bridges, and tunnels stretched throughout the empire, from Scotland to Mesopotamia. To this day, some of them remain in use, attesting to the quality of Roman engineering.

Paul and the synagogue

Traveling in Roman times, however, was not without its challenges. Sea travel, preferable because it was cheaper and less exhausting than land travel, was subject to the availability of cargo ships traveling on desirable routes. It was also prone to storms and shipwrecks, especially during the winter (cf. Acts 27:9–44; 2 Corinthians 11:25). As for land travel, there was the possibility of being assaulted by robbers because of scant protection outside cities (cf. 2 Corinthians 11:26) and the difficulty of finding a decent place to sleep at night. The *cursus publicus* (public way), a network of state-run stations used for courier and transportation services, was a lodging option for wealthy travelers; regular inns did not always enjoy good reputations, both in quality and morals. Sleeping by the roadside was

Paul's illness in Galatia

Paul says in Galatians 4:13 that it was "because of a physical infirmity" that he "first announced the gospel" in Galatia (NRSV). The construction "because of" (*dia* with accusative) cannot be softened to mean simply that the apostle became ill at some point during his first visit there, no matter how serious the illness was. Nevertheless, it is unclear how Paul's physical problem became the reason for his preaching of the gospel to the Galatians.

It is difficult to identify what kind of illness plagued Paul. Most interpreters rightly argue that his famous "thorn in the flesh," given to keep him humble (2 Corinthians 12:7), refers to the same situation because of the metaphor he uses next—that the Galatians were willing to tear out their eyes and give them to him (Galatians 4:15). It seems reasonable to conclude that the reference is to some persistent or periodically severe illness related to Paul's eyesight. See also Galatians 6:11 and Acts 23:1–5 (cf. Acts 9:8, 9).

sometimes the best option, which helps us understand why hospitality is encouraged in the New Testament (Romans 12:13; 1 Timothy 3:2; 5:10; Titus 1:8). In the case of gospel workers, they undoubtedly valued this spiritual gift (Romans 15:24).[5]

Hospitality was also a Jewish practice (Mark 6:10), and many synagogues had guest rooms for this purpose. This not only made it convenient for Paul to frequent synagogues on his journeys but also gave him direct access to God-fearing people who could then provide a bridge for reaching other Gentiles.

But the main rationale behind Paul's practice was primarily theological. As a lifelong Jew, he understood his Damascus road experience as a conversion *to* Jesus Christ, not *from* the Jewish faith and its fundamental aspects. Though he experienced a radical change with respect to many of his religious concepts (cf. Philippians 3:4–11), he never understood this transformation in terms of leaving one religion and embracing another.

Organized Christianity did not yet exist as a separate entity, so for most Jews, including preconversion Paul, the followers of Jesus were just another radical sectarian movement (Acts 9:1, 2). For most outsiders, including the Roman authorities, the differences between Christians and Jews were an internal Jewish affair (Acts 18:12–16). This scenario would change only after the Great Fire of Rome in A.D. 64. The inferno, which historians suspect Nero ordered, cleared the land for a new palatial complex, the Domus Aurea. Nero subsequently targeted Christians in his effort to diffuse blame, ordering them to be tortured and executed.

As for the early Christians, they believed themselves to be the true holders of the traditional Jewish faith and hope (Acts 2:22–24). Paul was persuaded that he had been called by the God of Israel who had always demanded exclusive worship. For him, faith in Jesus Christ was not a desertion of Jewish monotheism (1 Corinthians 8:6); it was a logical extension of his understanding of God. He remained loyal to the Jewish Scriptures and consistently drew his theological concepts from the history and literature of Israel, not from the history and literature of the Greeks.

He came to the Gentiles determined to share the richness of God's revelations to Israel (Romans 15:27), not to translate the Jewish faith into terms of Greek thinking. Though he spoke and wrote in Greek, the vocabulary and key concepts of his thought were biblical and developed with particular attention to Israel's religious history (2 Corinthians 3:7–18). It should be noted, however, that his forays into this history do not indicate a radical discontinuity between the Old Testament and the new era of salvation. In Galatians, for example, he reflects on the specific transitory role performed by the law within the old covenant (Galatians 3:19–25; 4:1–7, 21–31), knowing full well that the law transcends that role (Romans 7:12–14), does not contradict the enduring principles of the Abrahamic covenant (Romans 3:31; Galatians 3:21), and is not invalidated by the grace of salvation (Romans 3:3).

Paul never compromised his belief in Israel as God's covenant people (Romans 3:1–4; 11:1–5), even as the Gentiles began to outnumber Jews in the faith (cf. Romans 11:11–32). Though he no longer conceived of Israel's election in a narrow sense, he did believe that Israel's role in salvation history granted them priority in the preaching of the gospel (Romans 1:16). This was not only Paul's understanding; it was the priority Jesus envisioned in His Acts 1:8 commission to the disciples.

Paul's attachment to the synagogue, therefore, was not just for logistic and pragmatic reasons. He remained a faithful Jew; and wherever there was a Jewish community, he was convinced that the principle of "first to the Jew, then to the Gentile" (Romans 1:16, NIV) applied. It was only after the Jews expressly rejected the gospel that he would turn to the Gentiles (Acts 13:46, 47; 18:6; 28:25–28). Nevertheless, his "heart's desire and prayer to God" (Romans 10:1, NIV) yearned for the conversion of the Gentiles and their help in bringing more Jews to Jesus (Romans 11:14, 23, 26).[6]

Concluding remarks

Paul's first journey established him as the leading missionary among the apostles. Such recognition, however, is only part of the story. From the beginning, enormous difficulties and supernatural forces worked against him and Barnabas. They encountered Elymas, the Jewish sorcerer and false prophet in Paphos (Acts 13:6–12; cf. verse 10). John Mark deserted them and returned to Jerusalem (verse 13). Slanderous Jews kicked them out of Pisidian Antioch (verses 45, 50). Paul was stoned, dragged out of Lystra, and left for dead (Acts 14:19). At every turn, he risked his life for the sake of the gospel (Acts 15:26).

God never promised an easy path for Paul, and trials never diminished his missionary zeal (cf. Acts 14:21–26). Upon returning to Syrian Antioch, he and Barnabas "gathered the church together and reported all that God had done through them and how he had opened a door of faith to the Gentiles" (verse 27, NIV), a door that would never shut.

---

1. Gabriel Audisio, *Preachers by Night: The Waldensian Barbes (15th-16th Centuries)*, trans. Claire Davison, Studies in Medieval and Reformation Traditions (Leiden: Brill, 2007), 34.

2. Josephus, *The Antiquities of the Jews* 7.3.3.

3. Ellen White, *Testimonies for the Church*, vol. 5 (Mountain View, CA: Pacific Press®, 1889), 386.

4. Everett Ferguson, *Backgrounds of Early Christianity*, 2nd ed. (Grand Rapids, MI: Wm. B. Eerdmans, 1993), 82.

5. The Greek verb used in such passages is *propempō*, which means "to help/send on one's journey." The help in question included everything that might have been necessary, such as food, clothing, and money. Frederick William Danker, ed., *A Greek-English Lexicon of the New Testament and Other Early Christian Literature*, 3rd ed. (Chicago: University of Chicago Press, 2000), 873.

6. On Romans 11:26, see chapter 13 of this book.

The Jerusalem Council

Acts 15:1-35

"We believe it is through the grace of our Lord Jesus
that we are saved, just as they are."
—Acts 15:11, NIV

The horrors of World War II shocked the world. Besides the twenty million military casualties, it is believed that more than fifty million civilians lost their lives, including nearly six million Jews who were killed in the Holocaust. Hannah Arendt, a political philosopher from a secular German Jewish family, was one of those deeply touched by the war and, in *The Origins of Totalitarianism*, discusses how humanity could have reached such a low point.

Although much remains unexplained, the political situation in Europe after World War I was not ideal. Arendt describes how several countries underwent significant border changes, with some areas rearranged more than once. In the midst of such developments, certain groups were left without a country, while others had their citizenship revoked. These groups, called displaced persons, had nowhere to go and no government willing to find a solution for them. They could not be deported, for where would they be deported to? They could not be assimilated into a new country, for who would want to receive them and process the hundreds of thousands of citizenship applications? Without the protection of a government or higher institution, who would represent and defend their interests?

They were left to the mercy of the police, who tried to

handle the situation by force. With no country and no constitution, anything they did could be considered a crime, and any illegal action on the part of the police toward them was ignored by the government. Without protection, the "displaced persons" became a people without rights and, ultimately, without identity.[1]

The first Gentile converts to Christianity encountered a similar problem. In the ancient world, religion was intimately linked to cultural identity. There was no separation between one's secular and religious life. Gentiles who decided to accept Jesus as their Savior were thus faced with a dilemma: in giving up their former gods, they were leaving behind their former identities. At the same time, without circumcision, they were not considered Jews. Since the church was still essentially Jewish, this meant their conversion was not accepted, compromising the idea of salvation by faith alone. Soon after Paul's first missionary journey, the time was right to discuss this important issue.

Conversion and circumcision

The gospel message can be summarized in three simple statements. The first is that Jesus died for us, taking the punishment for our sins on Himself (2 Corinthians 5:21). Every human being is a sinner, and the wages of sin is death (Romans 6:23).

Second, if Jesus died for our sins, then salvation is through faith (Romans 1:17). The inability of our works to save us means there is nothing we can do to gain salvation. All we can do is believe in Jesus' substitutionary death; a death that signaled the gravity of sin and established the integrity of God's character in saving humankind (Romans 3:24–26).[2]

Third, if salvation is through faith, then it is equally available to all (2 Corinthians 5:15). The gospel demands impartiality: no one is privileged, and no one is excluded. God plays no favorites (Acts 10:34, 35), and His favor cannot be earned by human virtue or accomplishment. To think differently is to honor human pride, obligate God to us, cheapen His grace, and nullify His death (Romans 3:27; Galatians 2:21; 5:4; cf. Romans 4:14).

This third point, and by implication the other two, was the great challenge Paul faced with some of the Jewish believers. When news of his and Barnabas's mission reached Jerusalem, some believers came down to Antioch and contended that no Gentile could be saved without first converting to Judaism. It is important to remember, however, that the Jews in general did not believe a Gentile had to become a Jew in order to achieve salvation, whereas the Jews were expected to observe the entire corpus of the Mosaic laws (cf. Galatians 5:3). Some rabbis taught that righteous Gentiles, such as those who lived according to God's universal laws, would have a share in the world to come. Such laws, it was argued, were given first to Adam and again to Noah and thus binding upon all humanity. Though the first explicit reference to the Noahide laws, as they are known, comes from the second century A.D., it is possible the tradition behind them is much older. According to Scripture, however, righteous Gentiles are not those who observe the laws of Noah but those who observe the natural law, written in the human heart by the Spirit of God (Romans 2:14–16).

Apparently, the issue in the early church was not whether Gentiles could inherit a place in the coming world but whether they could be received into the church fellowship without becoming proselytes in the Jewish sense. It should be remembered that the first believers were Jews who did not think of themselves as forming another religion apart from Judaism. For them, everything hinged on circumcision.

As for the other two proselyte initiatory rites—baptism and a sacrifice in the temple—the first was required by the church from all its converts, even Jewish ones (Act 2:38, 41; 8:12, 36–38). Noncompliance with the second did not invalidate conversion or prevent full standing in the religious community; it only hindered participation in a sacrificial meal. This was particularly helpful in the case of those proselytes who lived in foreign countries, far away from the temple.

Circumcision occupied a central place in Jewish cultural and religious identity. It was the sign of the Abrahamic covenant, the sign that made them children of Abraham and of God Himself (cf. John 8:33, 39). To be circumcised not only validated one's standing as a Jew but also brought distinction from the world of unclean, godless people.

Interaction with Hellenistic culture, however, brought strong pressure against circumcision. Romans and Greeks considered it a barbarian practice. And since public nudity was common in social activities such as sport competitions and public baths, the Jews were confronted with shame and reproach on a daily basis. Sometimes, in specific political or financial situations, Jews were forced to pay higher taxes or even face the death penalty because of their circumcision. This caused some Jews to abandon Judaism completely. Others found ways to make circumcision more acceptable to the Gentile world; they would try to hide or conceal it by means of an operation called an epispasm, in which the foreskin was restored, or by cutting off such a small piece of the foreskin that it would be nearly unnoticeable.

Others, however, mostly in Palestine, adopted an even more rigid stance in support of circumcision. In what amounted to a protest against the threats of Greek culture, many came to view the practice as synonymous with salvation itself; something that keeps one under the dominion of God and ensures His blessings and participation in heavenly worship. To be uncircumcised, on the other hand, was to belong to "the children of destruction" who are destined to be slain and "rooted out of the earth," not to the children of the Abrahamic covenant (Jubilees 15:26, 34; cf. Testament of Levi 6:3; Community Rule 5:5; Thanksgiving Hymns 18:20). An example of this strong belief can be seen during the Maccabean period, when Mattathias and his band are said to have torn down pagan altars and forcibly circumcised all the uncircumcised boys that they found within the borders of Israel (1 Maccabees 2:45, 46).

The Jewish believers who opposed Paul's gospel certainly belonged to this third group. They came to be known as

Judaizers. Some of them were converted Pharisees who acknowledged Jesus as the Messiah but still equated circumcision with inclusion in the community of faith (Acts 15:5). In their view, uncircumcised Gentiles, even if they had been baptized, would still lie outside the covenant and never enjoy the privileges of true (Jewish) believers. Their conversion was illegitimate, and fellowship with them, whether social or religious, was considered unlawful (cf. Galatians 2:11–14). The implications were obvious: salvation was not for all, and faith was not enough—a complete repudiation of the gospel (cf. Galatians 1:6–9).

The meeting at Jerusalem

These were the undercurrents in Christianity under the umbrella of Judaism. The first-century social and religious context saw no separation between secular and religious life. Everything was connected: in the Greco-Roman world, deities were worshiped and honored at public festivities, allegiance to the emperor cult was expected of every citizen, and every family had household gods. Sacrifices celebrated births and coming-of-age ceremonies. Wealth and power were attributed to the favor of the gods. Even seemingly private events such as meals were often a type of offering to the gods. In this context, Gentiles who accepted Christ as their Savior would be faced with the dilemma of giving up much of their former identities. No longer could they participate in public idolatrous festivities, bringing into question their standing as citizens. Ties to their families would be compromised since they could no longer show the allegiance to the ancestral gods.

Were it not for circumcision, converted Gentiles would not necessarily have had bad feelings about joining Judaism. Even though Jews were considered inferior by most Romans, their religion was still acknowledged as possessing a strong identity of its own. Its antiquity, monotheism, and unique lifestyle were some of the factors that made it respectable to the Greco-Roman mind. It was a *religio licita*, a religion authorized by the empire, and so benefited from concessions that allowed for its free practice. Yet its insistence on circumcision for Gentiles placed the new converts in a religious predicament; one in which leaving their former gods, cults, and way of life was still not enough to have their conversion recognized. The practice of restricting salvation to Jews and advocating the necessity of human intervention (circumcision) represented a huge distortion of the gospel message for Paul, Barnabas, and the other Hellenistic believers who had established themselves in Antioch (cf. Acts 15:2; Galatians 2:4, 5).

To their credit, the attitude of the church in Antioch was exemplary. They decided to consult the church in Jerusalem and work on a joint solution that would preserve both the integrity of the gospel and the unity of the church. After some debate and shared testimonies (Acts 15:4–11), the council recognized that God had clearly accepted the Gentiles even though, from a Jewish standpoint, they lacked the prerequisites for conversion. The conclusion of Peter's speech strongly supported the message Paul had been preaching: "We believe it is through the grace of our Lord Jesus that we are saved, just as they are" (verse 11, NIV). If God had accepted the Gentiles' faith, who were they to impose restrictions upon them?

Yet the council did decide that Gentile converts should abstain from four things: (1) meat sacrificed to idols in pagan rituals, (2) blood consumption, (3) meat of strangled animals, meaning their blood had not been completely drained, and (4) all forms of sexual immorality. Although Christians would agree that sexual immorality should be avoided, the other three regulations are often considered a temporary accommodation intended only to facilitate Gentile-Jewish relations within the church.[3]

In reality, this decision, reached under the guidance of the Holy Spirit (verse 28), reflected the regulations found in Leviticus 17 and 18 concerning resident aliens—foreigners who chose to live in Israel (Hebrew: *gērim*).[4] Following such regulations meant that the foreigners had renounced paganism (Leviticus 18:30), addressing the core issue behind the council's decision. In the Greco-Roman world, paganism permeated nearly every aspect of life, and any Gentile wishing to join the

One in Christ

Both in the Jewish and the Greco-Roman societies, everything was a matter of division. Money meant power and authority, so working classes were lower in the social hierarchy. Women were inferior to men, children inferior to women, and slaves were lowest of all. And of particular import to Christianity was the issue of how to relate to foreigners and to people of different religions.

These social differences affected how people treated one another and resulted in contempt toward those of unequal rank. Christianity took a unique approach to this subject. It was not necessary to eliminate all social differences or to embrace a new social status in order to live together in harmony. Jews could continue being Jews, and Gentiles could continue being Gentiles (1 Corinthians 7:17–20).

In Christ, these social divisions were breached, and all, Jews and Gentiles, women and men, free and slaves, could live and worship in unity, despite their differences (Galatians 3:27–29; Ephesians 2:14–16; Colossians 3:10, 11).

church would have to take a clear stand against it.

This, however, was only the beginning of life as a Christian. Once the decision had been made to relinquish all pagan conventions and follow Jesus, the believer was supposed to live a life according to God's will (Romans 6:15–19, 22). In the pre-Christian era, it was no different with the *gērim*. Once admitted to the community, they should keep the Sabbath (Exodus 20:10; 23), participate in the religious festivals (Deuteronomy 16:11, 14), and fast on the Day of Atonement (Leviticus 16:29). They were allowed to enter the covenant of faith (Deuteronomy 29:10–15; 31:12) and offer burnt offerings (Leviticus 17:8; 22:18; Numbers 15:14–16). In sum, they, no less than the Israelites, were expected to be loyal to God (Leviticus 20:2; cf. Ezekiel 14:6–8). Circumcision was required only of those who wished to celebrate Passover

(Exodus 12:48, 49), thus fully identifying themselves with the Israelites (cf. Numbers 9:14).

The decision reached by the Jerusalem Council, known as the apostolic decree, recognized that being a Christian did not necessarily equate following the Jewish lifestyle and religious practices. Circumcision was not mandatory; neither were the Mosaic ceremonial laws, which were no longer valid because they had found their fulfillment in Christ (Hebrews 10:1–18). The same, however, cannot be said of the Sabbath, the dietary laws of Leviticus 11, and the other moral commandments pre-dating Sinai. They transcended God's covenant with Israel and were not intrinsically ceremonial (Genesis 2:1–3; 7:2; 26:5; Exodus 16:4, 5, 22–30; cf. Exodus 16:28).

The apostolic decree did not do away with these laws, nor did it initiate a new ethical order for the people of God (Romans 3:31). It did imply, however, that all were accepted by God, regardless of whether they were Jews or Gentiles. Just as the resident aliens were to be treated with love and fairness in Israel (Leviticus 19:33, 34), so were Jews and Gentiles to love and accept one another. "For in Christ Jesus neither circumcision nor uncircumcision counts for anything, but only faith working through love" (Galatians 5:6, ESV).

Concluding remarks

The decision reached by the Jerusalem Council was an important step in the right direction, but the problem was complex and far from being resolved. On one hand, the Judaizers would not give up easily. On the other, Jewish beliefs and attitudes about circumcision were not fully addressed. Although Gentiles had been exempted, most Jewish Christians, including the apostles, still considered law keeping as crucial to their own salvation (Acts 21:20–25) and that fellowship with uncircumcised believers was to be avoided (Galatians 2:11–14).

The implications were obvious, and clear distinctions remained. There were two separate communities: Jews and Gentiles. There were two separate gospels: one by faith and one through works. This is not what Jesus envisioned for the church

(John 17:20, 21) and not what the gospel was all about (Romans 1:16). The attempt to make salvation reliant on human status or works of any kind pained Paul and became the church's earliest and most insidious heresy—a heresy that plagues the church to this day.

---

1. Hannah Arendt, *The Origins of Totalitarianism* (New York: Harcourt Brace Jovanovich, 1973), 267–302.

2. On Romans 3:24–26, see Wilson Paroschi, "The Cross and the Sanctuary: Do We Really Need Both?" *Ministry*, August 2014, 6–9.

3. See, e.g., John R. W. Stott, *The Message of Acts: The Spirit, the Church, and the World* (Downers Grove, IL: InterVarsity Press, 1990), 250.

4. On the *gērim*, see chapter 6 of this book.

CHAPTER 9

The Second Missionary Journey

Acts 15:36-18:22

"Do not be afraid; keep on speaking, do not be silent.
For I am with you, and no one is going to attack and harm you,
because I have many people in this city."

—Acts 18:9, 10, NIV

In reaction to a sermon I preached at a recent master of divinity graduation ceremony, an experienced Seventh-day Adventist pastor wrote me, expressing concerns with the professionalization of ministry and the adaptation of business management techniques to church leadership. He noted that two-thirds of the Sabbath preaching calendar was committed to the promotion of programs or events determined by the local division, union, and/or conference. Smartphone apps were being used to record the activities of a pastor and allowed direct assessment of his performance. And one conference even required pastors to follow priority assessment and implementation strategies suggested by a business world author.

Though no one questions a pastor's need for time-management skills and clear objectives, approaches relying on programs and events easily impoverish pastoral ministry and deprive it of the Spirit's guidance and power. An entrepreneurial mentality is aimed at productivity and leveraged for personal and political gain. The problem with this mind-set is that the church is not an enterprise and mission is not primarily a business. Corporate priorities do not necessarily translate to spiritual matters. The Holy Spirit works with a different agenda and at a different pace.

This is the primary lesson to be learned from Paul's second missionary journey, described in Acts 15:36–18:22. While the apostle was making efforts to consolidate the church's presence in Gentile lands, God was giving objective lessons on how a gospel worker should follow the Spirit's guidance, leaving the results with Him.

Back in Galatia

Luke's selective choice of events brings the apostle straight to Derbe and Lystra (Acts 16:1) in Lycaonia, in south Galatia. Some three years had passed since he had first visited there (cf. Acts 14:6–21). During those years, a young believer named Timothy became mature enough to leave his family and become one of the apostle's faithful and lifelong coworkers. Though Timothy's father was a Gentile, his mother was a Jewish Christian named Eunice. She may have come to the faith through the influence of her mother, Lois (2 Timothy 1:5), who was probably among Paul's first converts there. Despite being uncircumcised, Timothy knew the Scriptures from childhood (2 Timothy 3:15) and, as a Christian, had already earned the respect of local believers (Acts 16:1, 2).

Since the Jews reckoned Jewishness through the mother's line rather than the father's, Timothy was a Jew. That he had not been circumcised on the eighth day after birth, as required by the Law (Genesis 17:12; Leviticus 12:3), was probably due to his father's opposition, given that the Greeks in general rejected circumcision as a barbaric practice. To the Jews, however, circumcision was the greatest of all precepts. According to the rabbis, it was greater than the Sabbath,[1] because it was the sign par excellence of loyalty to the Abrahamic covenant. Knowing that Timothy, an uncircumcised Jew, would be forbidden to enter the Jewish synagogues under the charge of apostasy, Paul had him circumcised. Luke explicitly says this happened "because of the Jews" (Acts 16:3, NIV), and the account seems to suggest that Timothy's father had already passed away.

Paul's motivation for this was entirely practical and not contradictory to the gospel he preached. Furthermore, it did not violate the guiding principle that neither the circumcised nor the uncircumcised should change their condition at conversion (1 Corinthians 7:18, 19). In this passage, Paul is not focused on the circumcised and uncircumcised. He is concerned with circumcised Jews and uncircumcised Gentiles. Timothy, an uncircumcised Jew, was an exception to the norm and did not fit in either category. His lack of circumcision was a unique circumstance and posed a serious hindrance in the attempt to reach Jewish communities. Paul had no choice but to have him circumcised, especially since there is no evidence the apostle ever taught that Jews should forsake Moses and the command to circumcise their children, as he would later be accused of (cf. Acts 21:21). Were Timothy a Gentile, Paul's attitude would have been unthinkable, especially after the Jerusalem Council. Moreover, the way he refers to Titus, an uncircumcised Gentile, in the context of the council (Galatians 2:3; cf. verses 2–9) shows he was unwilling to make

The Visigothic Code

The following confession, added to the Visigothic law codes in A.D. 681 by King Erwig, a complete puppet of the bishops, was sometimes used to make a Jewish convert show loyalty to the church:

"I hereby renounce all the rites and observances of the Jewish sect, and, without reserve, express my utter abhorrence of all their ceremonies and solemnities which I have practiced and kept in former times, until now; and I pledge myself that I will, hereafter, observe none of said rites or ceremonies, nor will adhere to any of my former errors; that is to say, I will not retain them in my mind, or, in any way, carry them into effect. Henceforth, renouncing all things which are condemned and prohibited by the doctrines of Christianity."*

---

* *Leges Visigothorum* 12.3.14.

concessions when the truth of the gospel was at stake (cf. Romans 3:28–30; 4:9–12; Galatians 5:2, 3, 11).

By having Timothy circumcised, Paul showed that his polemics against circumcision, especially in Galatians, had a definite bearing on salvation theology. His concept of freedom allowed him to behave like a Jew among the Jews in order to win them (1 Corinthians 9:19, 20). In other words, for utilitarian reasons, Paul could circumcise a coworker who came from a mixed marriage, as in Timothy's case. His understanding of circumcision is found in 1 Corinthians 7:19: "Circumcision is nothing, and uncircumcision is nothing" (NRSV; cf. Galatians 5:6; 6:15).[2] That is, since it makes no difference whether or not a man has been circumcised, circumcision could be used in the service of the gospel, provided it was not conditional to salvation. For Paul, accepting circumcision in an attempt to be made right with God meant a forfeiture of the saving benefits of Jesus' death (Galatians 5:2, 4).

The story of Timothy brings us face-to-face with an important issue: the gospel does not require Gentiles to become Jews, nor Jews to become Gentiles. In later Christian history, the acceptance of Gentiles in their original status was taken as validation of their alleged superiority. The destruction of Jerusalem and the massacre of the Jews by the Romans in A.D. 70 and again in A.D. 135 were viewed as evidence of God's abandonment. The remaining Jews, scattered all over the Christian world, were marginalized and treated with contempt. Jewish customs were deemed carnal, not spiritual. Circumcision became illegal and, together with the Sabbath and Levitical food laws, was said to have been imposed on the Jews because of their sins. The Hebrew Bible was called the *Old* Testament, implying it was of less value to Christians. Like Judas Iscariot, Jews were considered dishonest and greedy traitors, cursed by God, and forever guilty of having killed the Son of God. If baptized, Jews were expected to renounce all their ties with Jewish life, including Sabbath observance and dietary restrictions. It became something of a heresy to suggest that one could be both Jewish and Christian at the same time. In fact, the Second Council of Nicaea in A.D. 787 came to the point of explicitly forbidding Jewish believers to live as Jews (Canon 8). This was a complete reversal of Paul's teaching.

Paul never argued that Jews were to become Gentiles when they accepted Jesus. On the contrary, he taught that no one should change his condition (1 Corinthians 7:18). He never sought to dismiss differences between Jews and Gentiles in the sense of a Christian assuming a new, hybrid identity that replaces or combines the former ones.[3] His assertion that Jew and Gentile, slave and free, male and female "are all one in Christ Jesus" (Galatians 3:28, NIV) and that they have been clothed with "the new self" (Colossians 3:10, NIV) does not mean such differences have been removed (cf. 1 Corinthians 7:17–24); they simply do not divide anymore. Discrimination is gone. Exclusivism is gone. Every person is now reconciled with one another and with God through the Cross (cf. Ephesians 2:14–16).

Led by the Spirit

After finishing his journey through south Galatia, Paul, along with Timothy and his other companions, wanted to travel to Asia, a wealthy and highly civilized province (Acts 16:6). Ephesus, the largest and most important city of the province, was probably the apostle's intended destination. This seems reasonable because in his first journey he had already been in Pamphylia, to the south (Acts 13:13; 14:24, 25), and Bithynia was a little farther north. With a population of more than a third of a million, Ephesus housed the great temple of Artemis (in Latin, Diana), one of the seven wonders of the ancient world. This temple, along with other temples and sanctuaries, made Ephesus an important religious center, and its large Jewish population could certainly enhance Paul's evangelistic possibilities.

But God had different plans for him, and the Holy Spirit prevented the apostle from going that way (Acts 16:6). Next he considered going north, to Bithynia, which was the second most obvious choice, but again the Spirit did not allow it (verse

7). Since it appears Paul did not want to go back, the only option he had was to pass by Mysia and go down to the seaport of Troas, from where he and his group could sail in a number of directions (verse 8). Upon reaching Troas, God showed him in a night vision that they were to cross the north part of the Aegean Sea and head to Macedonia, in what is today's Europe (verse 9).

It is not clear why God directed Paul to Macedonia, because in his third journey the apostle would spend three years in Ephesus (Acts 19:1–21; cf. Acts 20:31). Additionally, the evangelistic results in Macedonia and Achaia, the province Paul visited next, did not seem to have been any better than in other places. This is particularly true of Athens, where, from a human perspective, the results could not have been worse (Acts 17:32–34). Also, the evangelization of Corinth and the establishment of the church there was marked by profound internal division and a number of other problems. Corinth and its affairs troubled Paul and occupied a considerable share of his attention, especially during his third journey. This is demonstrated by the length and frequency of his correspondence with the Corinthians. They wrote him at least once (1 Corinthians 7:1), and Paul wrote them three, if not four, letters (cf. 1 Corinthians 5:9; 2 Corinthians 7:8). For unknown reasons, only the second and the fourth letters have been preserved.

To human eyes, this indicates that the journey through Macedonia and Achaia, as opposed to the one through Asia, seems to have brought no outstanding benefit to Paul or the church. The results were not stellar, and the apostle continued to have problems with Jews because most of them did not accept the gospel (Acts 17:5–9). There was also an escalation of difficulties with the Roman authorities (Acts 16:19–24, 35–39; 17:6–9; 18:12–17). Yet this was God's plan; and though it could be argued that God had special plans for Corinth (cf. Acts 18:9, 10), this does not explain why Paul could not have preached the gospel first in Asia or Bithynia. What we see in Luke's account, particularly in Acts 16:6–10, is a "keen interest in the dialogue between human purpose and divine purpose, indicating that Jesus' witnesses, too, must patiently endure the frustration of their own plans in order to discover the opportunity that God holds open. This opportunity may not have been the next logical step by human calculation."[4]

Paul's example of following the Spirit's leading has powerful implications for the modern gospel worker. Life is packed with professional and personal obligations. There are programs to implement, projects to begin, goals to reach, visits to make, and counseling to do. No wonder pastors complain they have no time to study for sermons and help the church grow in faith. Add to this the prevailing entrepreneurial mentality and its pressure for results, and it is easy to see how following the Spirit becomes difficult. Yet few things can be so detrimental to Christian ministry as a lack of the Spirit's guidance.

By human standards, Paul's preaching at the Areopagus in Athens was a great failure (Acts 17:18–34). He was not trying to win the approval of people, but of God (Galatians 1:10), and he knew that God operates on the basis of divine considerations (cf. Acts 28:25–27). Paul's sense of obligation to people was such that he would not choose his audience (Romans 1:14; cf. 1 Corinthians 9:16). He would not try to reach only barbarians and the foolish just to gain better results and bolster his résumé. He would go wherever the Spirit led him and leave the results with God, knowing that irrespective of how much he or anyone else could do, it was God who gave the growth (1 Corinthians 3:6, 7).

Perhaps this explains his emphasis on the call to preach rather than a call to baptize (1 Corinthians 1:17; cf. 1 Corinthians 9:16). Methods and programs have their value but should never limit the Spirit's involvement in shaping pastoral ministry. And the Spirit is not concerned with status, recognition, and political gain. Abandoning quantifiable strategies, in deference to the leading of the Spirit, runs counter to human ambition. Such action would likely destroy proof of one's own investments of time, money, and energy. The fear is either of meager results, which will ruin the annual report, or in case they are plentiful, that the whole credit goes to the Spirit. Not rarely, church mission becomes cover for one's own political ambition.

On the basis of 1 Corinthians 2:1, 2, it is sometimes argued that Paul's more philosophical approach at the Areopagus was mistaken, possibly explaining his poor performance there. Two points, however, need to be clarified. First, Paul's approach there was perfect for his audience. The Council of the Areopagus, the most venerable institution in Athens, included wealthy, learned, and secular people—representatives of the city's elite. In modern terms, they could be described as materialists and rationalists, hardly representing ordinary people. For them, statues and temples were mere superstition or works of art. Having no knowledge of the Hebrew Scriptures, they would not have been reached with Paul's appeal to sacred history and Jesus as the promised Messiah. What worked in the Jewish synagogue of Pisidian Antioch would not have played well at the Areopagus (Acts 13:16–51).

For this reason, Paul chose to speak about the true knowledge of God in a way that was appropriate for his audience. He was not more intentional about "Jesus Christ and Him crucified" as in Corinth (1 Corinthians 2:2, NKJV) because he was not given the chance. He seems to have been interrupted the very moment he mentioned Jesus' resurrection from the dead (Acts 17:31, 32); the Greeks believed in immortality, not in resurrection (verse 32). The small number of converts in Athens, therefore, comes as no surprise. The situation is analogous to our attempt to reach postmodern societies. Significant results are not expected, but like the Greeks of old, they are entitled to hear the gospel (cf. Romans 1:14).

Second, 1 Corinthians 2:1, 2 does not allude to Paul's Areopagus address. This passage belongs to a section (1 Corinthians 1:18–2:5) in which the apostle unpacks his statement in 1 Corinthians 1:17b, that preaching "with eloquent wisdom" (NRSV) was not part of his calling. Describing his first visit to Corinth, Paul boldly reminds his readers that he purposely avoided lofty words and impressive wisdom to talk about the mystery of God (1 Corinthians 2:1). By this, he meant that the effectiveness of his evangelism was not bound to style or human wisdom. In fact, any response to the gospel should spring from the message itself, not from the aesthetic form of its presentation. Human wisdom and eloquence have the potential of rendering the Cross pointless (1 Corinthians 1:17).

The gospel excludes human boasting (verses 28, 29), while wisdom and eloquence exalt human talent and achievement. The latter puts hearers at risk of having their attention diverted from the Cross to the speaker's personality (1 Corinthians 2:5). The gospel originated with God (Galatians 1:11), and whenever it is preached in His power (Romans 1:16), He will make it fruitful (1 Corinthians 3:6, 7). He does this through the Holy Spirit (Romans 15:19; 1 Corinthians 2:10–16), without the help of human wisdom and rhetoric. Strategies, programs, and events that seem to provide a "competitive" edge can block divine activity and empty the gospel of its power (1 Corinthians 1:17).

Concluding remarks

"Connection with a church," Ellen White says, "does not take the place of conversion. To subscribe the name to a church creed is not of the least value to any one if the heart is not truly changed."[5] Conversion can be produced only by God (John 16:8–11), and divine activity in the human heart cannot be measured. Strapping the church's mission and pastoral ministry with a focus on numbers does no justice to the Spirit's role in conversion. On the contrary, it diminishes His sovereignty and drains the gospel of its power. This dishonors God and weakens the church with the ingress of unconverted people.

Pressure to baptize by constraint rather than conviction is misguided and can lead to the evaluation of pastors on the basis of their "productivity." To be truly successful, the work of the church must first be a spiritual endeavor, fueled by a genuine expectation of Jesus' soon return.

Church mission should never justify the adoption of evangelistic procedures that undermine the spiritual condition that is necessary to meet Jesus in peace. Paul's second journey is a solemn reminder that the Holy Spirit is crucial for individuals and the church. What began with the outpouring of the Spirit and was nurtured by His guidance will finish in His power (Acts 1:8).

---

1. Mishnah Nedarim 3:11.

2. Gerd Lüdemann, *Early Christianity According to the Traditions in Acts: A Commentary* (Minneapolis: Fortress Press, 1989), 176.

3. R. Kendall Soulen, *The God of Israel and Christian Theology* (Minneapolis: Fortress Press, 1996), 169.

4. Robert C. Tannehill, *The Narrative Unity of Luke–Acts: A Literary Interpretation*, vol. 2, *The Acts of the Apostles* (Minneapolis: Fortress Press, 1990), 195.

5. Ellen White, "The Truth as It Is in Jesus," *Review and Herald*, February 14, 1899, 1.

CHAPTER 10

The Third Missionary Journey

Acts 18:23-21:16

"I do not count my life of any value to myself, if only I may finish
my course and the ministry that I received from the Lord Jesus,
to testify to the good news of God's grace."
—Acts 20:24, NRSV

Fascinating conversion stories sometimes take a miraculous turn on biblical truths discovered in Scripture, timely evangelistic literature, or a providential broadcast. This was the case with Seventh-day Adventism's introduction in Brazil. In 1884, small packages containing Adventist literature were apparently sent from Germany and distributed among German immigrants who had settled in Santa Catarina, a state in the southern part of the country.[1] Wilhelm Belz and his family were among those who periodically received such literature and, by 1890, came to the Sabbath truth and started keeping it. In 1893, the first missionaries arrived in Rio. Two years earlier, some of them had been sent by the General Conference to work in Uruguay and Argentina, where there were also a number of German settlements.

In Rio, they gave Bible studies to Albert Bachmeier, a German sailor who recently converted to Protestantism, and invited him to join them as a colporteur. Though not yet baptized, Bachmeier came to Santa Catarina to work among the German settlers. Here he encountered the Belz family, who, along with a few others, had been quietly observing the Sabbath for about four years. In June 1895, the first Adventist pastor, Frank H. Westphal, was sent by the General

John's and Christian baptisms

Christian baptism derives from John's baptism, not from Jewish proselyte baptism. Except for its form (immersion), John's baptism was fundamentally different from all purificatory baths of Judaism in that it was moral (i.e., a "baptism of repentance for the forgiveness of sins," Mark 1:4, ESV; cf. Luke 3:3; Acts 13:24; 19:4), unrepeatable, and passive, in the sense that the people were baptized by John, rather than actively immersing themselves into the water (cf. Matthew 3:14, 16; Mark 1:8, 9; Luke 3:21; John 1:25, 28, 31; 3:23; 10:40).

As for Christian baptism, the New Testament clearly speaks of it in parallel to John's baptism (John 3:22, 23; 4:1, 2). Even after Pentecost, Christian baptism could still be defined as a baptism of repentance for the forgiveness of sin (Acts 2:38; 22:16; cf. Ephesians 5:25–27; Titus 3:5–7).

The two new elements that were introduced—administration in the name of Jesus and the gift of the Spirit (Acts 2:38; 8:14–17; 10:47, 48; 19:5, 6)—did not change its moral character (John 3:5; Acts 2:38–40; Romans 6:4, 5; Titus 3:5–7).

On the contrary, they only added a sense of belonging or personal commitment that was absent from John's baptism (1 Corinthians 1:12, 13) and the divine influence of the Holy Spirit in the believer's life, meaning that God is now really experienced as present and active (Galatians 4:6; 5:22–25; cf. 1 Corinthians 12:3).

Conference and arrived in the small village of Gaspar Alto, near Brusque. He baptized twenty-three people, including Bachmeier, and organized the first Brazilian Seventh-day Adventist church.

In Paul's third missionary journey (Acts 18:23–21:16), something similar happened. When he finally made it to Ephesus, he discovered a group of about twelve believers who seemed to live at the fringe of mainstream Christianity, lacking an acquaintance with important aspects of the Christian faith. Here he also had harsh confrontations with paganism and managed to pen a letter to the believers in Corinth (1 Corinthians 16:8). This book represents his strongest attempt to teach Gentile converts about the boundaries and requirements of their new life in Jesus, vis-à-vis their former pagan ways.

Ministry in Asia

On his return from the second journey, Paul made a short stopover in Ephesus, where he left Aquila and Priscilla (Acts 18:18–21), who were a Jewish couple he had met in Corinth (verses 1–3). These lifelong friends and fellow workers for the gospel centered their work on preparing the field for Paul's future labors on his next journey there.

While Paul was still traveling to Ephesus (cf. verse 23) however, a Jewish believer named Apollos came to the city. A native of Alexandria, Egypt, he was eloquent and well versed in Scripture, (verse 24).

> Meanwhile a Jew named Apollos, a native of Alexandria, came to Ephesus. He was a learned man, with a thorough knowledge of the Scriptures. He had been instructed in the way of the Lord, and he spoke with great fervor and taught about Jesus accurately, though he knew only the baptism of John. He began to speak boldly in the synagogue. When Priscilla and Aquila heard him, they invited him to their home and explained to him the way of God more adequately.
>
> When Apollos wanted to go to Achaia, the brothers and sisters encouraged him and wrote to the disciples there to welcome him. When he arrived, he was a great help to those who by grace had believed. For he vigorously refuted his Jewish opponents in public debate, proving from the Scriptures that Jesus was the Messiah.
>
> While Apollos was at Corinth, Paul took the road

through the interior and arrived at Ephesus. There he found some disciples and asked them, "Did you receive the Holy Spirit when you believed?"

They answered, "No, we have not even heard that there is a Holy Spirit."

So Paul asked, "Then what baptism did you receive?"

"John's baptism," they replied.

Paul said, "John's baptism was a baptism of repentance. He told the people to believe in the one coming after him, that is, in Jesus." On hearing this, they were baptized in the name of the Lord Jesus. When Paul placed his hands on them, the Holy Spirit came on them, and they spoke in tongues and prophesied. There were about twelve men in all (Acts 18:24–19:7, NIV).

That Apollos was a follower of Jesus is clear from the way Luke refers to him: "He had been instructed in the way of the Lord, and he spoke with great fervor and taught about Jesus accurately" (verse 25, NIV). Yet he knew only John's baptism, which probably meant he was an early disciple. After Pentecost, Christian baptism differed from John's in that it was administered in the name of Jesus and was associated with the gift of the Spirit (Acts 2:38; 8:14–17; 10:47, 48).

After being baptized by John, Apollos would have become acquainted with Jesus and, like some of Jesus' first disciples (cf. John 1:35–42), transferred his allegiance to Him. But he would have moved away from Palestine, probably back to Alexandria, sometime before Pentecost.

In the first century A.D., Alexandria was a major center of the Jewish dispersion.[2] Two of its five quarters were inhabited by Jews. Likewise, there was a sizable community of Alexandrian Jews in Jerusalem (cf. Acts 6:9), and it is credible that relocations from one city to the other continued during the time of the apostles.

The hypothesis of Apollos being an early disciple who had missed Pentecost seems reasonable. It would explain why Aquila and Priscilla gave him further instruction when he arrived in Ephesus. Though being able to show from Scripture that Jesus was the Messiah of Israel (Acts 18:28), Apollos needed to be updated on the developments in Christianity since the time of Jesus. Aquila and Priscilla also gave Apollos a recommendation letter addressed to the churches in Achaia (verse 27), allowing him to have an effective ministry in Corinth (1 Corinthians 3:4–6; 4:6; 16:12).

Apollos's account is connected with the account of the twelve men Paul met upon his arrival in Ephesus (Acts 19:1–7) and should guide our interpretation of it. (The chapter division as we have it, separating both accounts, is not the work of Luke; it was introduced as late as the thirteenth century and is not to be considered part of the canonical text.) The textual problem is shrouded in difficulty; because those men had not yet received the Spirit and knew only John's baptism, many interpreters have suggested they were residual followers of John the Baptist.

Nevertheless, by referring to them as "disciples" (verse 1) and believers (verse 2), Luke certainly wants his readers to understand them as Christians. When not otherwise specified, as in this passage, *disciple* in Acts always refers to a follower of Jesus (Acts 6:1, 2, 7; 9:1, 10, 19, 26, 36, 38; 11:26, 29; 13:52; etc.), and the verb *to believe* always points to Jesus as the object of faith (Acts 2:44; 4:4, 32; 5:14; 8:13; 9:42; 10:43; etc.). Also when Paul asked, "Did you receive the Holy Spirit when you believed?" (Acts 19:2), his question to them was not related to the person or the object of their faith; it addressed only their reception of the Holy Spirit when they first believed (Acts 19:2). Such a question would hardly make sense if the apostle was not addressing believers in Jesus.

This leaves two possible interpretations. First, their situation was analogous to Apollos's in that they would have been former disciples of John the Baptist, coming to faith in Jesus during His lifetime and then possibly moving away from Palestine, thus missing Pentecost and the outpouring of the Spirit.[3] Or second, they were converts of Apollos who had received only the baptism of John—or a baptism like John's—due to the fact that it was the only baptism Apollos knew and practiced.

This second alternative is preferable for the following reasons: (1) it explains why those disciples did not know anything about the Spirit, which would have been incredible if they were former disciples of John since, according to the Gospels, the Holy Spirit was part of John's prophetic proclamation (Matthew 3:11, 16; Mark 1:8, 10; Luke 3:16, 22; John 1:32, 33; Acts 1:5; cf. Luke 1:15); and (2) it clarifies why Paul baptized them again. There is no record of Aquila and Priscilla doing the same to Apollos.

Historically speaking, the validity of John's baptism could not be denied. To do so would be equivalent to denying the preparatory nature of his ministry (cf. John 1:6–8, 22, 23, 33, 34; 3:28), as well as the pre-Pentecost roots of the Christian movement (cf. Acts 13:24, 25). Thus, even though several of Jesus' disciples had most likely been baptized by John (John 1:35–42), as Jesus Himself had (Matthew 3:13–17), none of them needed to be baptized again after Pentecost.

From the pre-Pentecost perspective, there was nothing wrong with John's baptism. After Pentecost, however, such baptism, which was both prophetic and temporary by nature (Acts 19:4), was inadequate and needed to be replaced by the proper Christian baptism—a baptism that was now performed in the name of Jesus and included the gift of the Spirit. For this reason, while Apollos's own baptism by John remained valid, his baptizing of the twelve men with John's baptism was problematic and out of harmony with their place in redemptive history. Thus, their baptism by Paul was not rebaptism, but rather it was the legitimate baptism for post-Pentecost believers.

Two additional points are worth noting. The first has to do with the gift of tongues. After their baptism by Paul, the disciples received the Spirit, spoke in tongues, and prophesied (verse 6). This supernatural experience was their personal confirmation of being incorporated into mainstream Christianity or an indication that they were Christian missionaries, like Apollos, who were now enabled to bear witness to Jesus wherever they went.[4]

The second point relates to their baptism by Paul. Their encounter with the apostle should not be treated as a case of conversion. They were already Christians, and Christianity was not yet divided into different denominations. In fact, it was perhaps a unique situation in the apostolic church, in which an early disciple who had likely separated himself from the Jesus movement in Palestine was still performing John's baptism years after Pentecost.

Interactions with paganism

On the first journey, Paul and his companions seem to have followed a specific plan.[5] They would go to important cities, preach in the local synagogues, gather those who believed into new congregations (home churches), and then move on. Since most of their audience came from Jews, Jewish proselytes, and God fearers around the synagogues, it appears their purpose was to remain only long enough to establish a new congregation. On the second journey, the same pattern can be noted until Paul came to Corinth, where he stayed for a year and a half (Acts 18:11).

The change was not accidental. Up until then, except for a few isolated episodes (cf. Acts 14:8–18; 17:16, 17), the apostle had not yet undertaken significant efforts to reach pagans, but in Corinth he decided to be more intentional toward them. This would naturally require more time.

Besides its strategic location as a hub city for both land and sea travel, Corinth was a dynamic pagan center that attracted visitors from everywhere. People suffering from various diseases would flock to the temple of Asclepius, the god of healing, and his daughter Hygieia, the goddess of health. Every two years thousands of people would attend the Isthmian Games, held in honor of Poseidon, the god of the sea. The games began with a sacrifice, and then all participants had to swear on the altar that they would play by the rules. Entertainment surrounding the event included an abundance of alcohol and prostitution.

Not surprisingly, Corinth had a long-standing reputation for immorality and licentiousness. Roman geographer Strabo says that a thousand ritual prostitutes once served the Corinthian temple of Aphrodite,[6] and hordes of sailors and other travelers used to climb up to the temple for its rituals of orgy and inebriation. Among the Greeks, the term *corinthiazesthai*, which literally means "to live a Corinthian life," was used to describe immoral and degenerate behavior. In addition, Corinth was home to other temples of traditional Greek and foreign gods, such as the Egyptian gods Isis and Serapis. All of this presented a special opportunity for Paul.

On the third journey, things were not much different in Ephesus, where Paul stayed for three years (Acts 20:31). Located on the west coast of Asia and with more than a third of a million inhabitants, Ephesus was the largest and most important city of the province. In addition to its commercial and cultural significance, Ephesus was perhaps even more dominated by paganism than Corinth. Along with a number of other temples, it housed one of the most popular shrines of antiquity—a shrine dedicated to the fertility goddess Artemis, worshiped by the Romans as Diana. It contained an image of the goddess that was believed to have fallen from heaven (cf. Acts 19:35). From around the Mediterranean, pilgrims would come to the Artemision for numerous rituals and festivities (verse 27). This great temple, four times the size of the Parthenon in Athens, was, according to Pausanias,[7] the largest building of antiquity and one of the seven wonders of the ancient world. Ephesus was so intimately associated with magic and exorcism that books of magic recipes and incantations were often referred to as "Ephesian books."

Due to Paul's fervent evangelistic commitment (Romans 1:14), he would not confine his efforts to the synagogues and those attending them. In Ephesus, it seems he felt the challenges of paganism even more intensely than in Corinth (cf. 1 Corinthians 16:8, 9). According to Luke, an initial success in converting people from their belief in magic accompanied the apostle's labors there, and many willingly destroyed their magic books (Acts 19:13–19). Sometime later, however, a local silversmith named Demetrius, a maker of votive miniature silver niches of Artemis for visitor trade, organized a riot against Paul and his associates. Filling the almost twenty-five thousand–seat amphitheater of Ephesus with devotees of the goddess, people repeatedly cried out for nearly two hours, "Great is

Artemis of the Ephesians!" (verse 34, NIV). Were it not for the help of friends, the apostle could have been killed in the uproar (verses 29–31).

An important socioreligious aspect of Paul's time was that, no matter how idiosyncratic a particular religion was, it had the right to exist provided it was ancient, ancestral, and showed respect for other gods. Celsus, a second-century Greek philosopher and opponent to Christianity, remarked about the Jews that they "observe a worship which may be very peculiar, but it is at least traditional. In this respect they behave like the rest of mankind, because each nation follows its particular customs."[8] The problem with the Jews, however, was their refusal to acknowledge other gods, insisting that their God should be the sole recipient of worship (Exodus 20:3). It was this attitude of religious exclusivism, offensive to pagan contemporaries, that attracted the most criticism.

As a devout Jew, Paul was strongly monotheist. It is natural that he would show no consideration for pagan gods (1 Corinthians 8:4–6). In fact, he scorns them and wants his Gentile believers to break any possible links with idolatry and immorality (1 Corinthians 5:1–5, 9–11). In a time when religion was an innate part of one's identity, this message represented a huge challenge for new converts. Though not required to convert to the religion of the Jews through circumcision, they had to renounce all idolatrous practices and convert to the God of the Jews, thus becoming "servants of the living and true God" (1 Thessalonians 1:9, NJB; cf. Galatians 4:8, 9).

By demanding this, Paul conformed to the decisions of the Jerusalem Council (cf. Acts 15:29), except that he would not necessarily censure a Gentile convert for eating food, in a home setting, that had previously been sacrificed to idols and then sold in the market (1 Corinthians 10:25–27). Though fully rejecting the idea espoused by some of the Corinthians that it was acceptable to partake of idol meat at a pagan temple (verses 14–22), the apostle saw no problem with eating such meat at home, even at the home of an unbeliever (verse 27)—unless, of course, this offended someone's conscience (verses 28–33).

To clarify the issue, 1 Corinthians 8–10 and probably Romans 14 and 15 are not about unclean meat but temple meat. Not menu, but venue, as a New Testament scholar puts it.[9] And the reason Paul balked at sharing in sacrificial meals at pagan temples is that this would signify taking part in the sacrifice itself (1 Corinthians 10:18). Even if idols are nothing, worshiping them is a serious sin, equivalent to worshiping demons, and not suitable for a believer's participation (verse 20). It is wrong, the apostle adds, to eat at the Lord's table and also at the demons' table (verse 21). Doing so is an insult to God and rouses Him to jealousy (verse 22; cf. Exodus 20:5).

Concluding remarks

Paul's second and especially third journeys were marked by increasing incursions into the domains of paganism. From an ethical standpoint, it was more difficult to bring a Gentile to faith than a Jew, yet the apostle never lowered the standards or requirements to smooth his evangelistic efforts (cf. Galatians 1:10). He insisted that only the God of Israel was to be worshiped and that his Gentile converts should separate themselves from all forms of idolatry.

Such insistence ultimately came from the first table of the law (Exodus 20:3–11), and though Paul was against any attempt to attain salvation through the law, it is incorrect to say he preached a law-free gospel (cf. Romans 2:12; 7:7, 12; 8:4; 13:8–10; 1 Timothy 1:8–10). He never resigned his loyalty to the only "living and true God" (1 Thessalonians 1:9, NIV; cf. Romans 3:30; 1 Corinthians 8:4–6; Ephesians 4:6; 1 Timothy 2:5) and never accepted anything less from his converts. Nevertheless, the Jews were not fully convinced of Paul's orthodoxy, and upon Paul's return to Jerusalem from this third journey, the apostle's ministry would suffer a major setback.

---

1. The literature—initially a few volumes of the magazine *Stimme der Wahrheit* (Voice of truth)—was produced in Battle Creek, Michigan, but it is not clear whether it came straight from the United States or through Europe. According to the traditional story, it came from Germany through the influence of an immigrant who would have returned to Europe and then, having met some Adventist

missionaries, provided them with names and addresses in Brazil for the shipment of the packages. Floyd Greenleaf, *Terra de Esperança: O Crescimento da Igreja Adventista na América do Sul*, trans. Cecília Eller Nascimento (Tatuí, SP: Casa Publicadora Brasileira, 2001), 25.

2. Everett Ferguson, *Backgrounds of Early Christianity*, 2nd ed. (Grand Rapids, MI: Wm. B. Eerdmans, 1993), 381.

3. See Wilson Paroschi, "Acts 19:1–7 Reconsidered in Light of Paul's Theology of Baptism," *Andrews University Seminary Studies* 47, no. 1 (2009): 73–100.

4. See Ellen White, *The Acts of the Apostles* (Mountain View, CA: Pacific Press®, 1911), 283.

5. Some of the following thoughts are based on Dan P. Cole, "Into the Heart of Paganism," *Christian History* 14, no. 3 (1995): 20–24.

6. Strabo, *Geography* 8.6.

7. Pausanias, *Description of Greece* 4.31.8.

8. Origen, *Against Celsus* 5.25, quoted in Paula Fredriksen, *Augustine and the Jews: A Christian Defense of Jews and Judaism* (New Haven, CT: Yale University Press, 2010), 390n10.

9. Ben Witherington, *The Acts of the Apostles: A Socio-Rhetorical Commentary* (Grand Rapids, MI: Wm. B. Eerdmans, 1998), 466.

CHAPTER 11

Arrest in Jerusalem
Acts 21:17-23:35

The following night the Lord stood near Paul and said,
"Take courage! As you have testified about me in Jerusalem,
so you must also testify in Rome."
—Acts 23:11, NIV

The year was 1982. Brazilian pastor Ronaldo de Oliveira and his wife and one-year-old son arrived in Angola as missionaries. Pastor Oliveira was to be the new director of Bongo Training Mission School, which then had 140 students. The facilities included a hospital, a press, and an elementary school. For seven years, the country had suffered civil war, which would continue intermittently for another twenty years.

On the same day that Oliveira arrived at Bongo, the school was assaulted by one of the guerrilla groups fighting for power. He and his family, along with three other missionaries serving the hospital, were taken hostage. School personnel were forewarned of the rebels' advance, and a simple phone call could have delayed the missionary family for a day or two in Luanda, the capital city, preventing their capture. Since their arrival on campus on that day was much anticipated, it was thought that the rebels could easily learn about their absence, thus fear of retaliation prevented the phone call from being made.

For the next thirty-seven days, Oliveira and his wife, Rosemari, took turns carrying little André in their arms. Along with the other hostages, they were forced to walk through jungles, mountains, and even rivers, frequently traveling at night to hide their movement. For another five days, they were trucked to a type of concentration camp, close to the Namibian border. Here they were kept in a small room and, after intense diplomatic effort, were liberated two months later.

Altogether, they traveled more than one thousand miles, mostly on foot and in the dark. Twice the group was intercepted by government troops. There was heavy gunfire and several casualties, but all the prisoners were miraculously protected.

At the end of his third journey, Paul was also arrested, not in the mission field but in his "hometown" where he was known as a devout Pharisee (Acts 23:6). His capture was not by a guerrilla group but by his own fellow countrymen and not because of money but because of his commitment to the gospel. Sadder still, with their opposition and bitter feelings toward Paul, was the role of the apostles and church leaders in Jerusalem.[1] Fortunately, this was not the end of his ministry because God still had plans for him (verse 11).

Judea in the midfifties

When Paul began his missionary journeys around A.D. 45, the Judean stage was being set for the events that culminated with the tragic destruction of Jerusalem in A.D. 70. Several developments fostering Jewish nationalism to dangerous levels were taking place in rapid succession, which seriously affected Paul himself. The Jews, of course, were never content with the idea of foreign rule, but Rome's official policy toward them was one of toleration, even allowing special privileges.

Judaism was acknowledged as a *religio licita*. The integrity of the temple precincts, the synagogues, and the sacred Jewish Scriptures was safeguarded. Provisions were made for Sabbath observance without interference. Coins minted in Palestine bore no images, even though it was nearly impossible to avoid coins with the emperor's portrait from circulating there (cf. Mark 12:16). As a rule, the standards of the Roman army, which carried images, were not displayed in Jerusalem, and the Jews were exempted from the cult of the emperor as long as they offered sacrifices in the temple on his behalf as a sign of loyalty.

Yet there was a huge gap between policy and practice. Unfortunately, the Roman officials serving in Palestine never understood the sensitive Jewish religious conscience. Even when motivated by good intentions, they failed to recognize the peculiarity of Jewish customs and beliefs that were radically different from anything else considered normal and commonplace in the vast Greco-Roman world. From the beginning, perhaps because it was a small and poor country, the provincial history of Judea shows the people had to endure some of the worst administrators Rome could provide. Conditions quickly deteriorated with the death of Herod Agrippa I in A.D. 44, just before Paul set off on his first journey through Cyprus and Galatia.

Three years earlier, in A.D. 41, Agrippa had become king of the reestablished kingdom of Judea. For nearly four decades, the country had been treated as a low-rank province, directly under the emperor's control and ruled through governors such as Pontius Pilate, whose official residence was in Caesarea. For all intents and purposes, Agrippa was a vassal of Rome, befriended and personally appointed by the emperor. Because he was a Jew through his father, he was granted some degree of independence and was able to reunite all Jewish territories. This made the Jews look forward to far greater things, such as their complete liberation from Roman rule. In Jewish tradition, Agrippa is held in high regard for his devotion to the law and the relevant services he performed for the nation. Nevertheless, he persecuted some Christians and even had the apostle James, the son of Zebedee, executed (Acts 12:1–4). His death is described in verses 20–23 as a punishment from God.

When Agrippa died, Emperor Claudius frustrated the Jews by returning Judea to the status of a Roman province; this time under a procurator also located in Caesarea. Anti-Roman feelings rose, and it was around this time that agitators known as Zealots increased their subversive activities. A severe famine in Judea between A.D. 46 and 49, predicted by a Christian prophet named Agabus (cf. Acts 11:27, 28), only intensified hatred towards Roman rule.

On one hand, many Jews would naturally relate the famine to the return of pagan oppressors to their country; on the other, robbery and plunder were common and were met with ferocity by the procurators. Tiberius Alexander (A.D. 46–48) captured and crucified James and Simon, the sons of a certain Judas the Galilean, for these crimes.

Arriving in the aftermath of the famine, the incompetent Ventidius Cumanus was the next procurator (A.D. 49–52). Under his leadership, one of the Roman soldiers placed at the temple court in Jerusalem to prevent any uprising during the Passover desecrated the sanctity of both the temple and the feast by exposing his bare genitals to the crowds. In the riot that followed, thousands of Jews were brutally killed. Not long after, during the siege of a small village near Jerusalem, another soldier found a copy of the Torah, tore it up, and threw it into the fire while uttering blasphemies. Both offenses became known all over the country, infuriating the Jews and intensifying the climate of hostility towards Rome—and Gentiles in general. In the wake of these atrocities, Cumanus was deposed by Claudius and called back to Rome in shame.

About this time, in A.D. 49, Claudius commanded all Jews, possibly those who were not Roman citizens, to be deported from Rome (cf. Acts 18:1, 2). According to Suetonius, the deportation was due to disturbances within the Jewish community instigated by a certain *Chrestus*,[2] believed to be nothing more than a misspelling of *Christus*, the Latin for "Christ." In this case, the disturbances were probably caused by the activities of Christian missionaries.[3] Despite having occurred in distant Rome, the episode almost certainly impacted Judea to some degree, adding to the brew that gradually sank the entire province into a cauldron of rebellion and factionalism.

Antonius Felix (A.D. 52–60), Cumanus's successor and perhaps the worst of the Judean procurators, inherited the social and economic problems created by the famine and responded to them with excessive violence. According to Josephus, it was impossible to calculate the number of robbers he crucified.[4] Together with his brother Antonius Pallas, Felix was apparently a freed slave of Antonia Minor, Claudius's mother. The fact he was appointed as procurator, a most unusual position for a freedman, suggests he enjoyed the special favor of the emperor, to whom he was also related by a former marriage. Such high position seems to have gone to his head, for he never missed an opportunity to show who was in charge. Tacitus says of Felix, "Practicing every kind of cruelty and lust, he wielded royal power with the instincts of a slave."[5] It was inevitable that Felix's repressive and violent policies would considerably add to the nationalistic and revolutionary fervor existing in Judea. Eventually, such fervor affected the believers in Jerusalem, particularly those closely related to the Pharisees (cf. Acts 15:5). In light of this, how would the people in Judea, believers included, have viewed the Hellenizing activities of Paul, the former Pharisee, among the Gentiles?

Paul must have been aware of this scenario when he sailed from Corinth back to Jerusalem at the end of his third journey. When writing to the believers in Rome around A.D. 57, he asked them to pray on his behalf for what could happen to him at the hands of the Judean rebels (Romans 15:30, 31). And during the short stopover in Miletus, just across the Aegean Sea, he shared with the Ephesian elders the Holy Spirit's warning that imprisonment and suffering might lie ahead of him (Acts 20:22, 23).

The collection for the poor

The situation in Judea threatened Paul's life and ministry but did not deter him from traveling there. He was driven by something more important than his own safety. He was focused on the unity of the church and was prepared to die for the gospel and the brotherhood between Jews and Gentiles within the community of faith (cf. Acts 20:24; 21:13).

Since the end of his first journey, the apostle began facing the threat of Judaizers who emphasized circumcision and the law as a whole for the salvation of Gentiles (Acts 15:1, 5; Galatians 2:4). In theory, the council of Jerusalem recognized that salvation was by God's grace (Acts 15:11); but as they were not willing to give up their convictions, Judaizers deepened their efforts against Paul and his gospel (Galatians 3:1). As for the other Judean believers, including the apostles, they had yet to fully recognize that salvation was by grace. They not only continued to emphasize the need of circumcision for Jews (Acts 21:20–25) but also refused to fellowship with uncircumcised Gentiles (Galatians 2:11–14). This treatment of the Gentiles as second-class believers created a division in the church.

This situation required that the Judaizers be vigorously confronted or the whole gospel was imperiled. God's grace would be nullified, Jesus' death would be rendered pointless (Galatians 1:6–9; 2:21), and the believers would still be under the yoke and power of sin (Galatians 2:4; 5:1). This is why Paul was so determined to go to Jerusalem despite all the risks. Besides earnestly wishing the salvation of his fellow Jews (Romans 9:1–5),[6] he had a gospel to defend and a church to build (Romans 1:1).

The Jerusalem Council is usually dated to A.D. 49, around the time the famine reached its peak. The year A.D. 48–49 was a sabbatical year, adding to the scarcity of food. In a sabbatical year, the land was to rest from cultivation, and if any produce grew by itself, it could be used for daily food by whoever needed it (Exodus 23:10, 11). Because of the prolonged drought, however, the poor would have little relief. Such a precarious situation, aggravated by the pooling of goods that followed Pentecost (Acts 2:44, 45), is the reason behind the request made to Paul, at the council, to remember the poor of the Jerusalem church (Galatians 2:10).[7]

Sensing an intensification of the animosity toward him and the Gentile believers, the apostle took advantage of this request to conceive a visionary plan that could supply financial aid to the brethren in Judea and at the same time "build bridges of love and understanding between the two separate branches of Christianity."[8] Paul refers to this as "the collection [or "ministry"] for the saints" (1 Corinthians 16:1, ESV).

The idea was simple. Giving was to be systematic and voluntary. In relation to the Corinthians, they were to set aside on the first day of the week a portion of their income, so that no collection would be necessary when Paul arrived. The money would then be sent on to Jerusalem through people chosen by the congregation, and the apostle would personally write letters of introduction for them. And if the Corinthians had no objection, he would travel with those who had been appointed for the mission (verses 2–4). In Macedonia, the recommendation seems to have been the same (2 Corinthians 8:1–7; cf. Romans 15:26, 27), and probably also in Galatia and Asia. When Paul finally left Corinth for Jerusalem, he was accompanied by representatives of all those regions (Acts 20:4).

The journey was not easy. Though resolved to stick with his plan, Paul was quite apprehensive about what could become of him in Judea (Acts 20:22, 23; Romans 15:30, 31). Quite a few fellow believers along the way tried to dissuade him from going there (Acts 21:4, 12), especially after Agabus's dramatized prophecy (verses 10, 11). Because of the unfavorable situation

On the first day of the week

Paul's instruction to the Corinthians to set aside part of their income on the first day of the week (1 Corinthians 16:2) is often cited in support of Sunday observance. Careful analysis of the passage, however, shows that such a conclusion is an attempt to read a different meaning back into the New Testament text.

There is nothing in the passage that suggests any sacredness attached to the first day of the week. Moreover, the passage says nothing about going to the church or bringing a weekly offering to the church's charities on that day.

A literal translation of Paul's words reads, "Let each one of you lay by him in store, as he may prosper" (ASV; cf. ESV, NASB, NKJV, NRSV, NJB), clearly indicating that the setting aside was to take place at home. The emphasis is clearly on personal stewardship rather than on faithful church attendance.

regarding Paul's ministry and gospel, both inside and outside the church, his chances were not good. Upon arriving in Jerusalem, his fears were confirmed. Luke does not mention the reception of the aid (cf. Acts 24:17, 18) but describes in detail the apostle's arrest and the Jews' conspiracy to take his life.

Two points about this story should be highlighted. First is the suggestion with which the church leaders met Paul. After raising doubts about his orthodoxy (Acts 21:20–22), they advised him to do something very Jewish in order to appease Jewish believers: sponsor the Nazirite vow of some Jewish-Christian pilgrims who had come to Jerusalem to celebrate Pentecost (verses 23–25). This vow was a special act of consecration that lasted thirty days and included a sacrifice in the temple (Numbers 6).

Second is Paul's own contribution to his arrest. Inexplicably, he yielded. Perhaps the psychological pressure was too intense for him, more than anything else he had endured in his ministry (cf. 2 Corinthians 11:23–27). Unfortunately, all heroes of faith have their flaws, as seen in the lives of Abraham, Moses, Peter, and others. It could be argued that Paul was just following his principle of becoming a Jew to the Jews (1 Corinthians 9:19–23). This time, however, it seems like a compromise because it signified his endorsement of the legalistic motives behind the recommendation.

The church leaders were not trying to protect Paul against the Judaizers. They were trying to protect their own interests and would be happy with the results if they could see the apostle capitulate. This might explain Ellen White's statement that "the Spirit of God did not prompt this instruction; it was the fruit of cowardice."[9] The implication of Paul's attitude was exactly the one he tried to oppose: there are two gospels, one to Gentiles, of salvation by faith, and another to Jews, of salvation by works. "He [Paul] was not authorized of God to concede as much as they asked."[10]

Complicating things further, Paul's attempt to please Jewish believers backfired. Because of the Gentiles who escorted him with the collection, he was thought to have introduced one of them (Trophimus, from Asia) into the inner court of the temple, where only Jews could enter (Acts 21:29). The real reason behind the accusation, however, was Paul's activities among Gentiles, considered by Jews and Jewish believers alike as wholly contrary to some of the pillars of the Jewish religion (verse 28). When given the chance to speak, Paul's attempt to justify his commitment to the Gentiles (verse 21) was taken as an implicit confirmation of the charges raised against him. This angered the crowd and, perhaps even more than before, was a clear demonstration of the xenophobic mood then predominant in Judea (verses 22, 23). In the end, Paul was taken by Roman soldiers into the barracks (verse 34) and remained in Roman custody for about two years before being sent to Rome for trial (Acts 24:27; 25:12).

Concluding remarks

The collection for the poor had more than a philanthropic motivation. It had been carefully designed by Paul to stimulate unity within the church as a gesture of solidarity from Gentiles to Jews. Yet essential to such unity was a clear understanding of the gospel, its power (Romans 1:16), gratuitousness (Romans 3:22, 24, 28), and universality (verses 29, 30), which requires that all human works or privileges be excluded (verse 27).

The Judean believers strongly resisted this idea, also resisting the recognition of Gentile believers as sharing their same spiritual level. The nationalistic and revolutionary passion gripping Judea in the fifties only exacerbated their anti-Gentile sentiment. In such context, Paul's collection effort failed to achieve its intended result. In fact, it turned against the apostle and ended up causing his arrest in Jerusalem. This represented a major blow to his ministry—one that eventually cost him nearly five years of detention (Acts 24:27; 28:30) and forced him to change his missionary plans.

His long-awaited journey to Rome was canceled (Romans 1:11–13; 15:22–24; cf. Acts 19:21), yet not all was lost. In the midst of his deep anguish and desolation, Jesus Himself assured him he would still preach in the empire's capital (Acts 23:11).

And he did (cf. Acts 28:30, 31), though no longer as a free man.

———

1. Ellen White, *The Acts of the Apostles* (Mountain View, CA: Pacific Press®, 1911), 417.

2. Suetonius, *Divus Claudius* 25.

3. James D. G. Dunn, *Christianity in the Making*, vol. 1, *Jesus Remembered* (Grand Rapids, MI: Wm. B. Eerdmans, 2003), 141–143.

4. Josephus, *The Jewish War* 2.13.2; Josephus, *The Antiquities of the Jews* 20.8.5.

5. Tacitus, *Annales* 12.54.

6. On Romans 11:26, see chapter 13 of this book.

7. For the previous response of the Antiochene church to the famine mentioned in Acts 11:27–30, see chapter 4, note 2.

8. Paul Barnett, *Behind the Scenes of the New Testament* (Downers Grove, IL: InterVarsity Press, 1990), 190.

9. White, *The Acts of the Apostles*, 404.

10. White, *The Acts of the Apostles*, 405.

Confinement in Caesarea

Acts 24:1-26:32

*"Whether quickly or not, I pray to God that not only you
but also all who are listening to me today
might become such as I am—except for these chains."*
—Acts 26:29, NRSV

The course of history is punctuated by the extraordinary achievements of individuals who clung firmly to their convictions, opposed common patterns and mind-sets, and defended their claims in court. This is certainly true of Martin Luther, the sixteenth-century monk whose act of insurgence forever changed the development of Western society. By defending *sola Scriptura*, he launched the Protestant Reformation, radically influencing politics, culture, religion, dogmas, thinking, and language.

None of this, however, came without cost. Luther risked his clerical position, his reputation, and even his life in face of the accusations leveled against him at the Diet of Worms. Despite these challenges, he felt his "conscience" was "captive to the Word of God."[1] This description of Luther's struggle reminds us of Paul, who also faced fierce opposition to maintain and propagate his beliefs.

Like Luther, Paul also endured extreme conditions to honor the gospel truth. Even at one of the most crucial moments in his life, when taken to trial in the Roman imperial city of Caesarea, he still remained faithful to his duty and boldly witnessed to two Roman procurators (Felix and Festus) and a Jewish king (Agrippa II).

109

The similarity of Luther's and Paul's sagas is remarkable. Both were learned men of their time. Both were commissioned to challenge the prevailing systems. Both were sent to other cities for court hearings. Both appealed to the emperor. And both stood firm to the truth of the gospel. Though Paul's arrest had been precipitated by his own mistake in trying to please the believers in Jerusalem, God still had plans for him (Acts 23:11), and he would not renounce his calling.

Paul's trial

Paul's transfer to Caesarea for trial was providential. Though he had been arrested due to internal Jewish matters (cf. Acts 22:30; 23:28, 29), it soon became clear that he would not be tried fairly by the Sanhedrin and that his life was at risk if he stayed in Jerusalem. The Sanhedrin was the highest authority in Israel in religious and political matters. During a trial, the accused did not have a defense attorney and was responsible for calling his own witnesses. In order to secure a conviction, the Sanhedrin required the testimony of at least two witnesses.

In Luke's account, there seem to have been no witnesses; and after Paul's defense and the discussion among members of the court, some of those present acknowledged that they could find nothing wrong with him (Acts 23:6–9). Besides the lack of evidence for conviction, the Sanhedrin had no authority to inflict capital punishment (cf. John 18:31), and so, driven by their hate for Paul and his ministry, they began plotting to kill him in an ambush (Acts 23:12–15). Informed of this plot and aware that the prisoner was a Roman citizen (cf. Acts 22:27–29), the tribune made the necessary arrangements for him to be safely tried in Caesarea under the supervision of the Roman procurator (Acts 23:16–31). The extraordinary effort to ensure Paul's safe transfer (cf. verses 23, 24) is another indication of the mounting tension between Jews and Romans in Judea.

Caesarea was located about seventy miles northwest of Jerusalem. It was a beautiful city with an artificial port. Built by Herod the Great in 21 B.C., it was named after the emperor Caesar Augustus. It had a mixed population of Jews and

Gentiles, but the number of the latter far exceeded that of the former. When the Romans took full control of Judaea in A.D. 6, Caesarea became their administrative capital and home to the governor's official residence, the Praetorium. It was here that Paul was kept prisoner before his trial (verse 35).

It is important to note that throughout the book of Acts, Judea was a Roman province under a governor, a kingdom under Agrippa I, and then a province again under a procurator. At the time Paul was taken over to Caesarea, Felix was the procurator and responsible for judging his case.

Felix was not only immoral and corrupt, he was also repressive and violent, fueling nationalistic and revolutionary zeal in Judea. Upon entering office, he immediately managed to separate the Jewish princess Drusilla, daughter of Agrippa I, from her husband, King Azizus of Emesa, and take her as his third wife (cf. Acts 24:24). Another example of Felix's vicious character was the banishment of Eleazar ben Dinai, the Zealots' leader, in chains to Rome, while tolerating the much more dreadful Sicarii, who were political revolutionaries he used for his purposes. This group of Jewish rebels heavily opposed the Roman occupation of Judea. Felix is reported to have paid a large sum of money to induce the closest friend of Jonathan, the high priest at the time, to arrange for the high priest's murder by the Sicarii.[2] It was under the supervision of this man that Paul was to be tried.

The Roman procedures of judicial inquiry (Latin: *cognitio*) involved five steps: (1) the plaintiff comes before the administrative authority and reports his case; (2) the defendant is summoned; (3) the plaintiff prosecutes in the presence of the accused; (4) the accused presents his defense; (5) the judge, sometimes after consulting with his council, declares the verdict.[3] The trial was open to the public, and a scribe (Latin: *notarius*) would write up the minutes of the proceedings. Luke's account (verses 1–27) contains elements of such legal affairs. He divides the trial into three parts: (1) the prosecution (verses 1–9); (2) the defense (verses 10–21); and (3) the aftermath (verses 22–27).

Paul's accusers came down from Jerusalem, displaying impressive political and social credentials (verse 1). The high priest himself appeared, along with other elders, and their powerful position and status would have been beneficial if Felix was keen on maintaining peaceful relations with Judea's aristocracy. As a Roman citizen, however, Paul still had an advantage. This explains why, in order to convince Felix of their accusations against the prisoner, the Jews hired a professional orator named Tertullus (verse 1), whose eloquent speech reflects proficiency in forensic rhetoric and an awareness of Roman politics. After an acclamatory introduction (verses 2–4), Tertullus laid down the accusations against Paul (verses 5, 6). They were threefold: (1) Paul was troublemaker (literally, "a plague"; cf. ESV) and stirred up riots among the Jews; (2) he was a ringleader of the Nazarene sect; and (3) he had tried to profane the temple.

Being a troublemaker, which would be associated with rebellion and civil disturbance, was a capital crime in Roman legislation. This is similar to the charges brought against Jews during the reigns of Claudius and Nero, leading to severe repressive measures against them (cf. Acts 18:2). The allegation that Paul was the ringleader of a sect was not a religious charge but a political one (cf. Acts 21:38). Tertullus's rendering of the accusation insinuated that the sect of the Nazarenes was anti-Roman and politically dangerous. In light of Felix's violent policies, the overall concern of the Roman Empire to repress seditious groups, and the rising of nationalist spirit in Judea, these charges were serious and would appeal to Felix's bias against Jewish agitators.

The third accusation, related to the temple, was intentionally left unexplained. In the temple precincts, signs in Greek and Latin warned Gentiles not to enter the inner courts. Disobedience could result in the death penalty. Though being a Roman citizen, Paul was fully Jewish (Philippians 3:5) and was legally permitted to go beyond the outer court. When he was captured, the Jews accused him of defiling the temple (Acts 21:28), but Tertullus knew this accusation was not entirely valid and probably would not stick, which is why he formulated the charge only as an attempt, rather than an accomplished action (cf. Acts 24:6).

After hearing Paul's defense and working within his legal rights, Felix ended the trial without deciding Paul's fate (verses 22, 27). It would be tempting to say that, because of his relative acquaintance with the Christian faith (verse 22), Felix might have noticed exaggerations on the part of the accusers or inconsistencies between what was brought before him in court and Lysias's report (Acts 23:26–30; cf. Acts 24:22). But the real motive for postponing the verdict seems to have been wholly political. If he freed Paul, there would no doubt be a negative reaction from the Jewish leaders, possibly tainting his administration and leading to further revolts. On the other hand, if Paul was truly the ringleader of a popular Jewish movement spread throughout the empire (cf. Acts 24:5), a condemnation could also incite dissatisfaction among Paul's partisans.[4] Therefore, it seemed more convenient for the procurator to keep Paul in custody indefinitely, while also hoping to gain bribery benefits (verses 25, 26), which fits perfectly with what is known about Felix's character from extrabiblical sources.

After two years, Felix was succeeded by Festus (verse 27), and it was natural that the new procurator would try to establish good relations with the Jewish leaders (Acts 25:9). Though at first he did not give in to their request of bringing Paul back to Jerusalem (verses 2, 3), he still did not acquit him, even after Paul's self-defense and the Jews' failure to prove their accusations (verses 7, 8). Festus's disposition toward pleasing the Jews and accepting a change of jurisdiction would place Paul once again at the mercy of the Sanhedrin (verse 9), and the apostle reacted strongly, reiterating that he had done nothing worthy of being condemned by Jewish law. Fearing he would not be given a fair trial, he appealed to Caesar (verses 10, 11, 20, 21).

Roman citizens had the right to appeal to higher courts, including the emperor himself, if they felt they were not being treated fairly by the magistrate or if they had been wrongly sentenced to flogging, torture, imprisonment, or death. If the magistrate ignored such an appeal, he could be punished by death.

Appealing to the emperor, however, was not easy. The prisoner would need to personally cover the costs of travel to Rome and the living costs while awaiting trial. In addition, the prisoner would have to be financially responsible for bringing witnesses to Rome to support his case. Therefore, having the right to appeal did not guarantee it would actually happen. Average low-class citizens without financial means and personal connections in Rome would have a difficult time being heard by the emperor, and many did not even try to appeal.[5] Paul forged on by faith, relying on Divine Providence and the promise he had been given two years before, right after his arrest (Acts 23:11).

Paul's defense

Although Luke records only summaries of Paul's responses to the accusations leveled against him, in both of his speeches—before Felix (Acts 24:10–21) and later on before Festus and Agrippa (Acts 26:2–23)—the apostle establishes two main lines of defense: (1) he denies any wrongdoing on his part, and (2) he makes it clear that the real motive he was being judged by was Israel's hope in the resurrection of the dead. Before Felix, he questions the validity of Tertullus's case, arguing he had come to Jerusalem to worship, and it was in such condition he was caught by the Jews (Acts 24:11, 12; cf. verses 17, 18). Contrary to what Tertullus said (verses 5, 6), he was not disputing with anyone at the temple or stirring up people in the synagogues or anywhere else in the city. That no evidence could be produced against him was in itself an indication of his innocence (verse 13). Paul does not negate his faith in Jesus but vigorously opposes any suggestion that this was in disagreement with Jewish religious tradition (verse 14). He then raises two further points that were devastating to the accusers' case: (1) the absence of the Asian witnesses (verse 19), which had the potential of rendering the trial invalid, and (2) the fact that those who were there could speak only of his hearing before the Sanhedrin the week before (verse 20), and as such they had nothing to accuse him of, except that he believed in the resurrection of the dead (verse 21; cf. verse 15).

Before Festus and Agrippa, Paul presents much the same response, though in reverse order. He reviews his past life from the time he was a blameless Pharisee (Acts 26:2–5; cf. Philippians 3:5, 6), through his persecution and punishment of those who believed in Jesus of Nazareth (Acts 26:9–11), concluding with his Damascus road encounter and the commission he received from Jesus to be "a servant and a witness" among the Gentiles (verses 12–18; cf. verse 16, ESV). The bottom line of Paul's argument is that there was nothing in his record of service that disavowed his integrity and that his arrest was simply the result of his loyalty to God and the heavenly vision (verses 19–21).

At the close of his apology, Paul circles back to the reason for his arraignment: Israel's hope in the

The Greeks and the resurrection

In 1 Corinthians 1:23, Paul says that the gospel was "a stumbling block to Jews and foolishness to Gentiles" (NRSV). The main issue concerning the Gentiles was the resurrection, which was entirely uncongenial to the Greco-Roman mind (cf. Acts 17:31, 32; 26:23, 24). In Aeschylus's account of the establishment of the Areopagus court in Athens by the city's patron goddess Athena, Apollo said, "Once a man dies and the earth drinks up his blood, there is no resurrection."* The predominant belief at the time as to the state of the dead was the immortality of the soul, according to which the human soul is an immaterial and incorporeal substance that survives the death of the body. An exception was the Epicurean philosophers, who considered the soul to be made of atoms like the rest of the body, and that both body and soul end at death.

_____
*See Aeschylus, _Eumenides_.

resurrection of the dead (verses 6–8). This is a point he repeatedly emphasizes in his self-defense speeches. If he could be accused of anything, it was of sharing the Jewish belief in the resurrection, which for him had found its utmost fulfillment in Jesus Christ (Acts 23:6; 24:15, 21; 26:6–8; 28:20). In other words, it was his belief in the resurrection of Jesus that pointed to his fidelity to the Jewish faith.

In the Old Testament, whether understood metaphorically or realistically, the theme of the resurrection is closely connected with Israel's hopes. In several passages reflecting exilic conditions, the restoration of the nation is portrayed in resurrection terms (Isaiah 25:8; 26:19; Ezekiel 37:11–14; Daniel 12:1, 2; Hosea 6:1, 2). More broadly, the kingly Messiah promised to Israel is conceived as free from earthly corruption, and His kingdom, as everlasting (Psalm 16:10; Isaiah 9:6, 7; 11:1–12; Jeremiah 23:5, 6; Ezekiel 37:24–28; cf. John 12:34).

It is against this background that Paul's sermon in Pisidian Antioch is to be understood. There he proclaims the resurrection of Jesus as the fulfillment of the Messianic promise given to Israel (Acts 13:23, 30, 32–37; cf. Acts 2:24–29).[6] That is, central to the Messianic hope is the belief that God gives life to the dead, and central to the resurrection concept is the belief that Jesus was raised from the dead. And this is the great irony—and tragedy—of Paul's arrest and trial. In the final analysis, he was being judged only because he was proclaiming the fulfillment of Israel's dearest hope and expectation.

In his description of Paul's case to Agrippa, Festus revealed his surprise that the charges against the prisoner were not related to any capital offense, whether political or criminal, but had to do with matters concerning Jewish religion, in particular "a certain Jesus, who was dead, but whom Paul asserted to be alive" (Acts 25:19, ESV). This was the key issue; something the Jewish authorities tried to deny from the very beginning of the apostolic proclamation (Acts 4:1–3, 18; 5:27, 28; 7:54–58; 26:8–12; cf. Matthew 28:11–15). For the early Christians, Paul in particular, the resurrection of Jesus was the crucial event that secured the validity of the Christian faith and the continuity between Jews and Christians as God's covenant people (Acts 26:6–8). Additionally, it was also the crucial event behind Paul's ministry, for if Jesus had not resurrected from the dead, Paul's apostolic commission would be fraudulent (verses 13–19; cf. 1 Corinthians 15:8; Galatians 1:1, 15, 16).

Finally, the resurrection of Jesus is the crucial event that brings legitimacy to our salvation. For without it, His death would have no saving power, we would remain in our sins, and there would be no hope of future life (1 Corinthians 15:17–19). It is in this sense that Jesus is "the firstborn from the dead" (Colossians 1:18, ESV) or "the firstfruits of those who have fallen asleep" (1 Corinthians 15:20, ESV). To use a classical statement, "the resurrection of Christ is a pledge and proof of the resurrection of His people."[7] As George Ladd puts it, "If Christ is not risen from the dead, the long course of God's redemptive acts to save His people ends in a dead-end street, in a tomb. If the resurrection of Christ is not reality, then we have no assurance that God is the *living* God, for death has the last word. Faith is futile because the object of that faith has not vindicated himself as the Lord of life. Christian faith is then incarcerated in the tomb along with the final and highest self-revelation of God in Christ—if Christ is indeed dead."[8]

Concluding remarks

Paul's trial in Caesarea gave him the opportunity to demonstrate his innocence. But the final verdict was not rendered. Feeling like nothing more than a pawn in the hands of corrupt and capricious procurators, he decided to exercise his Roman rights and appeal to the emperor in Rome. Later, Festus and Agrippa would readily admit to each other that Paul had done nothing deserving imprisonment, much less death, and could have been set free had he not appealed to Caesar (Acts 26:30–32).

Based on this narrative, a casual reader could easily conclude that Paul's decision was mistaken, like the one that had precipitated his arrest in Jerusalem. But in fact, both dignitaries were willing to acknowledge the prisoner's innocence only after they had been conveniently relieved of responsibility for his case and freed from the threat of political fallout for granting him release or condemnation. In any case, Paul would be sent to Rome and given the opportunity to have his long-cherished dream fulfilled (Acts 19:21; cf. Romans 1:13; 15:22–24, 28, 29).

Whether Paul's decision was right or wrong, God's sovereign plan could not be stopped. Sooner or later, with or without going to Spain, as a free man or as a prisoner, through straight or tortuous paths, the apostle to the Gentiles would still bear witness to Jesus in the heart of the empire (Acts 23:11). Paul was not perfect, but his faith and commitment to God eclipsed his debilities (Acts 20:24; cf. 2 Corinthians 4:7–10; Philippians 3:12–16) and served to power the growth and establishment of Christianity.

---

1. Heiko Oberman, *Luther: Man Between God and the Devil*, trans. Eileen Walliser-Schwarzbart (New Haven, CT: Yale University Press, 1989), 39.

2. Josephus, *The Antiquities of the Jews* 20.8.5.

3. Ben Witherington, *The Acts of the Apostles: A Socio-Rhetorical Commentary* (Grand Rapids, MI: Wm. B. Eerdmans, 1998), 703.

4. Brian Rapske, *The Book of Acts in Its First Century Setting*, vol. 3, *The Book of Acts and Paul in Roman Custody* (Grand Rapids, MI: Wm. B. Eerdmans, 1994), 165, 166.

5. Rapske, *Book of Acts*, 55.

6. Robert C. Tannehill, *The Narrative Unity of Luke–Acts: A Literary Interpretation*, vol. 2, *The Acts of the Apostles* (Minneapolis: Fortress Press, 1990), 319.

7. C. Hodge, quoted in Leon Morris, *The Cross in the New Testament* (Grand Rapids, MI: Wm. B. Eerdmans, 1965), 258n134.

8. George Eldon Ladd, *A Theology of the New Testament*, ed. Donald A. Hagner, rev. ed. (Grand Rapids, MI: Wm. B. Eerdmans, 1993), 354.

Journey to Rome

Acts 27:1-28:31

"Do not be afraid, Paul; you must stand before Caesar."
—Acts 27:24, ESV

Because of his refusal to worship pagan gods, Ignatius, the bishop of Antioch, was sentenced to death and taken to Rome and was executed in A.D. 109, during Trajan's persecution. Escorted by ten soldiers while on the journey, he wrote letters to several churches along the way, thanking them for their love and prayers and offering counsel on other issues. The most striking aspect of his letters, however, was his eagerness to visit Rome despite the fate that awaited him. He counted it an honor to follow in his Savior's footsteps and emulate His suffering. Upon arriving in the imperial capital, Ignatius was taken to the amphitheater, most likely the Colosseum, where he was torn apart by wild beasts for the amusement of thousands of spectators.[1]

In A.D. 67, under Nero's persecution of the church, Paul was taken to Rome for execution. This was the apostle's second Roman imprisonment, alluded to in the pastoral epistles (2 Timothy 4:6–8). On the first trip, some seven years before, he must have been set free by Nero himself, due to the weakness of the charges against him. Luke, however, chooses not to mention Paul's liberation, simply mentioning that the apostle eventually came to Rome and, despite being a prisoner, conducted a fruitful ministry there (Acts 28:30, 31; cf. Philippians 1:12–14; 4:22).

The church in Rome

Accompanied by Luke and Aristarchus, Paul and other prisoners are sent to Rome under the custody of a centurion named Julius (Acts 27:1). Luke carefully describes the journey and increases the reader's interest in the apostle's plight. As Christ's ambassador, it is not surprising that Paul would share in His suffering. In this regard, note the parallels between Jesus and Paul: both are arrested by Jewish mobs and then handed over to Roman authorities (Luke 22:47–53; 23:1–5; Acts 21:10, 11, 27–36); both are confronted with false accusations (Luke 23:1, 2, 5, 10, 13, 14; Acts 21:28; 24:5–9); both are tried by the Sanhedrin (Luke 22:66; Acts 22:30–23:10), a Jewish king (Luke 23:6–12; Acts 25:13–26:30), and the local Roman administrator (Luke 23:1–3; Acts 24:1–23; 25:1–26:30); both are sentenced to be scourged at some point in their trials (Luke 23:16, 22; Acts 22:24); both are victims of hatred and prejudice (Luke 23:18–23, 35; Acts 21:35, 36; 22:22, 23; 23:12–15); both are found guiltless (Luke 23:4, 15, 20–22; Acts 23:29; 26:31, 32); and both receive unjust treatment for political reasons (Luke 23:18–25; Acts 24:24–27; 25:6–9). The foreboding narrative causes the reader to wonder, *Will Paul suffer Jesus' fate and be executed by the Romans to appease his Jewish enemies?*

Beyond these parallels, it should be remembered that Luke builds his narrative around the disciples' mission described in Acts 1:8: "You will be my witnesses in Jerusalem, in all Judea and Samaria, and to the ends of the earth" (NRSV). Of course, Luke knows Paul will make it to Rome and testify before the emperor (Acts 27:24), but the reader does not. Misfortunes plague the journey as Paul faces a violent sea storm (verses 13–20), starvation (verses 21, 33), shipwreck (verses 39–41, 44), soldiers who want to kill all the prisoners (verses 42, 43), a poisonous snake (Acts 28:3), and the prejudice of pagans (verses 3–5). Apparently, Luke offers the detailed and dramatic account to clarify that "come what may, God will fulfill his purpose by having Paul preach the good news in the very heart of the empire."[2]

Rome was the capital, the greatest city of the empire, and boasted a population of more than one million inhabitants.

Peter and the church in Rome

Fourth-century church historian Eusebius of Caesarea tells of Peter arriving in Rome to overthrow the work of Simon Magus (cf. Acts 8:9–24) in the second year of Claudius, around A.D. 42.*

The *Catalogus Liberianus*, a compilation of early church history dating from A.D. 354, also speaks of Peter as the founder of the Roman church, having exercised an episcopate of twenty-five years, until his death under Nero (A.D. 67).

Yet this is nothing more than a later legendary tradition that sought to explain where Peter went when he departed Jerusalem "and went to another place" (Acts 12:17, ESV).

As for Eusebius's notice, it is impossible to reconcile it with Galatians 2:7–9 (written several years after the Jerusalem Council in A.D. 49), according to which Peter was still in Jerusalem at the time of the council and had apparently not yet left Palestine, except to go to Syria, which is still on the east coast of the Mediterranean (verses 9–14; cf. Acts 15:6, 7).

More reliable traditions associate Peter (and Paul) with Rome only at the time of his martyrdom under Nero and because his mortal remains stayed in possession of the church there.†

---

* Eusebius, *Ecclesiastical History* 2.14.1–6; Eusebius, *Chronicle*.
† Ignatius, *To the Romans* 4.3; Irenaeus, *Against Heresies* 3.1.1; 3.3.2.

Founded in 753 B.C., it was at its apex in New Testament times. The proletariat packed multistory apartment buildings, and the aristocracy lavished revenues from across the empire on large suburban villas and country estates. The heart of the city, where the Roman Forum and the Imperial Fora were located, was furnished with an array of public buildings unequaled in any capital. It was the nerve center of ancient Rome, where people gathered for commercial, political, and religious affairs.

The origin of Christianity here is wrapped in mystery. The New Testament is silent on the subject, and the scant information found in extrabiblical sources is unreliable. Paul's first possible link to the Roman church is his friendship with Aquila and Priscilla during his time in Corinth around A.D. 51 (Acts 18:1, 2). They had left Rome because of Claudius's decree that evicted all the Jews from the city some two years before. Though it is not stated that they were already Christians, the narrative implies it and says nothing about Paul converting or baptizing them (cf. 1 Corinthians 1:14–16; 16:15, 19). Another link is his letter to the Romans, our earliest concrete reference to the presence of a Christian community in Rome. In this letter, written about A.D. 57, Paul acknowledges that the Roman church has existed "for many years" (Romans 15:23, ESV), placing its origins at the beginning of the apostolic period.

A recurring hypothesis connects the introduction of Christianity in the empire's capital with the events following Stephen's death. Acts states that among the Hellenistic Jews who were baptized at Pentecost, some were from Rome (Acts 2:9–11). Luke also mentions the existence of a "synagogue of the Freedmen [*libertinōn*]" (Acts 6:9, ESV) in Jerusalem, composed of Jewish slaves who had managed to attain their freedom in the Roman world. These former slaves could have come from anywhere in the empire, but many may have descended from Jews taken to Rome by Pompey as prisoners of war in 63 B.C., when the Romans first invaded Jerusalem. With the scattering of the Hellenistic believers during the persecution by Saul (cf. Acts 8:1), it is possible some returned to their homes of origin (cf. Acts 11:19–21). Hence, those from Rome could well have formed the nucleus of the Christian community in that city upon returning there.[3]

Some five years after meeting Aquila and Priscilla in Corinth, Paul decided he "must also see Rome" (Acts 19:21, ESV). In his letter to the Roman church, written shortly afterward, he outlines his plan to visit them on the way to Spain (Romans 15:24, 28, 29). Though he had never visited Rome (Romans 1:10–15;

15:22, 23), he had a fair knowledge of the church there and was personally acquainted with several believers (Romans 16:3–15); some of whom were his relatives (verses 7, 11). Others had worked with him before (verses 3, 7, 9) or had been converted through his own efforts elsewhere (verse 5). In addition, he seems to refer to five local home churches (verses 5, 10, 11, 14, 15), which were the basis of their association. Lastly, he is also well acquainted with the strengths and weaknesses of the church (Romans 1:8), most notably the difficult relations between the Jews and the Gentiles (Romans 14:1–15:13; cf. Romans 3:9, 29; 10:12).

Thus, even if the church in Rome had not been established by Paul, he still had considerable influence on the believer there, explaining their respect and appreciation. As he approached the city on his epic journey, he was met at different points by believers who had heard he was coming (Acts 28:15). Word of his plans had probably preceded him during his week in Puteoli, 170 miles south (verses 13, 14). Such demonstrations of love and care from his beloved friends heartened the apostle and helped him face his final trial by the emperor (verse 15).

In his official report to Caesar, Festus must have written that, according to Roman law, Paul was not guilty of any significant crime (Acts 25:26, 27; 26:30–32; cf. Acts 23:29). This explains why he was allowed to rent a private dwelling (Acts 28:30) instead of being sent to a regular prison or military camp. Following Roman practice, however, he remained chained to a soldier the entire time (verses 16, 20); and in this manner, he carried out his letter-writing ministry (cf. Ephesians 6:20; Philippians 1:7, 13, 17; Colossians 4:10, 18; Philemon 1:9) and bearing witness to Jesus Christ (Acts 28:31).

Paul's ministry in Rome

Soon after his arrival, following his policy of going first to the Jews (Romans 1:16), Paul invited the Jewish leaders to hear him state his innocence and explain his arrest (Acts 28:17–21). His purpose was to create an atmosphere of trust that allowed him to share the gospel. Intrigued by the allegations against him, the

Jews decided to give him a chance (verses 22, 23). As usual, the results were mixed: some believed, and some did not (verse 24). To express his disappointment, Paul quoted Isaiah 6:9, 10 to convey God's judgment on them because of their deliberate rejection of the gospel (Acts 28:26, 27). His conclusion—that God's salvation would then be taken to the Gentiles (verse 28)—can be misconstrued as the Jews having no further opportunity for conversion. But this passage only echoes previous statements by Paul (cf. Acts 13:46, 47; 18:6) that he would always turn to the Gentiles after having preached to the Jews of a certain locality.

All of this underscores a striking phenomenon related to Paul's missions—the progressive expansion of the gospel among the Gentiles on one hand, and its progressive rejection by most Jews on the other. This posed a theological problem as relevant then as it is today.

Three years before this episode in Acts 28, Paul felt compelled to address the issue, and it occupies three chapters of his epistle to the Romans (Romans 9–11). When Gentiles began outnumbering Jews within the church, it became impossible to avoid the question of whether God's plan for Israel had failed. The question seems to have been particularly significant in Rome, especially after Claudius deported the Jews in A.D. 49, as this exile also affected those who believed in Jesus, such as Aquila and Priscilla (Acts 18:2). Five years after Claudius's death (A.D. 54), the lapsing edict allowed the Jews to return, significantly impacting the composition and self-understanding of the Roman congregations. During the exile, the remaining Gentiles would have gradually become the majority, taking over leadership positions and distancing themselves from Judaizing and the legalistic way of life. On their return to Rome, Jewish believers would have been placed in the awkward situation of integrating with groups that felt foreign, if not hostile, to them. In such a scenario, tensions between the two groups emerged, spurred by the general anti-Gentile feeling existing among the Judean Jews.

This backdrop for Paul's letter to the Romans, and evidence within the letter itself, indicates the apostle was trying to help Jewish and Gentile believers better appreciate the gospel and its implications for their self-understanding in relation to one another. He reminds the Gentiles of Israel's election and priority in redemptive history (Romans 1:16; 3:1, 2; 9:4, 5; 11:28, 29), the Jews of the futility of works for salvation (Romans 3:20, 27, 28; 4:2–8; 9:11, 30–32; 11:6), and both of the universality of sin (Romans 2:12; 3:9, 19, 22, 23; 5:12), placing both on equal footing before God (Romans 1:16; 3:29, 30; 9:30–32; 10:12, 13). He unequivocally states that Jews and Gentiles are sinners in need of grace (Romans 3:24; 4:16; 5:2, 15–21; 11:5, 6). No one is privileged, no one is excluded, and no one should despise or judge another (Romans 14:1–4, 10, 13, 20–23; cf. Romans 15:1–7).

The success of the gospel among the Gentiles highlighted a growing concern in the fledgling church: What was Israel's place in salvation history? The gospel stands in continuity with the Old Testament (cf. Romans 3:21, 31; 4), and limited results among the Jews led to erroneous conclusions about their favored status before God. It is at this point that Romans 9–11 and Acts 28 intersect.

In his letter to the Romans, Paul makes three important points concerning Israel. First, the rejection of the gospel by most Jews does not mean God's plan for Israel failed. He can effectively work through the firstborn, which was standard procedure in a patriarchal society, or through a younger son to achieve His goals (Romans 9:6–13). The divine plan is not hindered by the firstborn's lack of faith, as in the case of Ishmael (verses 6–9; cf. Genesis 16; Galatians 4:23), or the renouncing of rights, as in the case of Esau (Romans 9:10–13; cf. Genesis 25:29–34). In both situations, God's election of Isaac and Jacob, even if revealed beforehand (cf. Genesis 25:19–23), was no arbitrary choice but the consequence of errant human decisions related to the older son.

God is not a hostage of human failure. The achievement of His purposes is independent of human will or exertion (Romans 9:16), and His actions should not be questioned (verses 20, 21). Though divine election is not based on human merit (verse 11; cf. Deuteronomy 9:4), when the response is inappropriate, God has the right, in His infinite mercy (Romans 9:14–18; cf.

Exodus 33:19), to make course adjustments that ensure the continuity of His plan (Romans 9:22–29). The unbelief of the Jews (the firstborn) became the opportunity for the Gentiles (the younger son) (cf. Romans 11:30), who were also children of Abraham, regardless of their biological descent (Romans 9:7; cf. Romans 4:16–18; Galatians 3:7–9; 4:25–28, 31).

The second point regards the Jews' rejection of the gospel. Blame for their denial of the Messiah (Romans 9:30–10:4, 14–21; 11:21, 22) could be placed on no one else, but that did not mean they were rejected by God (Romans 11:1, 2). Paul's conversion is evidence that Jews could be saved by grace and join the remnant of Israel (verse 5). Their salvation is a clear demonstration that God's mercy is at work among them and that all the Jews of Israel have not been cast out. God is more than able to save any Jew who comes to Him in faith (verses 23, 24).

The third and last point about the Jews in Romans 9–11 is Paul's hope that the conversion of Gentiles will contribute to the conversion of Jewish people (Romans 11:11–14). Apparently, a provocation to jealousy (verses 11, 14) would cause the Jews to repent and return to God (verses 14, 23). In other words, if Israel's failure became an opportunity for Gentiles (verse 30), Paul now wishes the conversion of Gentiles to be an opportunity for Israel (verses 26, 31).

Even today, the salvation of Israel is a charged topic, and it is important to remember that this is not a prophecy. Though there is no question that the apostle is talking about ethnic Israel, he is not anticipating a full inclusion of Jews at the end of time. It is true that several times in Romans 11 the future tense is used when referring to the salvation of Israel (verses 14, 23, 24, 26), but from the beginning of chapter 10, Paul makes it clear that this is but his "heart's desire and prayer to God" (Romans 10:1, ESV). In the original Greek of chapter 11, he refers to such salvation five times by using the subjunctive mood (verses 14 [2x], 27, 31, 32), expressing his wishes or some possibilities, not necessarily real actions. This matches verse 23, where he says that God has the power to graft the Jews back onto the olive tree "*if* they do not continue in their unbelief" (ESV; emphasis added).

Finally, no fixed time line is established for Israel's salvation. By using the word *now* three times in verses 30, 31, Paul seems to understand the preaching of the gospel to the Gentiles and the development of God's purpose for Israel as having a present fulfillment, within the framework of the present era of salvation—a work that was already in full progress (verses 13, 14).[4]

Concluding remarks

Eventually, Paul made it to Rome. Despite his prisoner status and the sad note about the Jews rejecting the gospel, the last scene of Acts is one of triumph and assurance (Acts 28:30, 31). It features the fulfillment not only of God's promise of Paul bearing witness to Jesus in that great city, even before the emperor (Acts 23:11; cf. Acts 9:15; 27:24), but also of the mission given to the disciples in Acts 1:8. Perhaps this is why Luke did not concern himself with mentioning Paul's release after the two-year imprisonment.

The apostle never left the Mediterranean and never went to Spain, as he wished. But in traveling to Rome, he stood at the crossroads of the Gentile world, just as Jerusalem was the center of the Jewish world. In this sense, by preaching the gospel in the empire's capital, Paul reached the ends of the earth and accomplished his Gentile mission. It was a strong beginning for Christianity, but much remains to be accomplished. Today, every believer has been promised the same Spirit that powered Paul's life and ministry. By God's grace, the results will be just as spectacular.

---

1. Bryan M. Litfin, *Getting to Know the Church Fathers: An Evangelical Introduction* (Grand Rapids, MI: Brazos Press, 2007), 44.

2. James D. G. Dunn, *Beginning From Jerusalem* (Grand Rapids, MI: Wm. B. Eerdmans, 2009), 998.

3. In Acts 28:21, 22, the Jews of Rome express ignorance only about Paul's activities, not necessarily about the presence of followers of Jesus in the city. What they say could well include local Jews who had come into contact with Christians, either in the city itself or elsewhere.

4. For further discussion, see Wilson Paroschi, "The Mystery of Israel's Salvation: A Study of Romans 11:26," *Ministry*, May 2011, 21–24, https://www.ministrymagazine.org/archive/2011/05/the-mystery-of-israel%E2%80%99s-salvation:-a-study-of-romans-11:26.

Recommended for further study

Barnett, Paul. *The Birth of Christianity: The First Twenty Years*. Grand Rapids, MI: Wm. B. Eerdmans, 2005.
————. *Paul: Missionary of Jesus*. Grand Rapids, MI: Wm. B. Eerdmans, 2008.

Bruce, F. F. *Paul: Apostle of the Heart Set Free*. Grand Rapids, MI: Wm. B. Eerdmans, 1977.

Carson, D. A., and Douglas J. Moo. *Introducing the New Testament: A Short Guide to Its History and Message*. Edited by Andrew David Naselli. Grand Rapids, MI: Zondervan, 2010.

Edwards, Judson. *Acts: Living With Passionate Faith*. Annual Bible Study. Macon, GA: Smyth & Helwys, 2008.

McRay, John. *Paul: His Life and Teaching*. Grand Rapids, MI: Baker Academic, 2003.

Patzia, Arthur G. *The Emergence of the Church: Context, Growth, Leadership, and Worship*. Downers Grove, IL: InterVarsity Press, 2001.

Peterson, David G. *The Acts of the Apostles*. The Pillar New Testament Commentary. Grand Rapids, MI: Wm. B. Eerdmans, 2009.

Phillips, Thomas E. *Paul, His Letters, and Acts*. Library of Pauline Studies. Peabody, MA: Hendrickson, 2009.

Porter, Stanley E. *Paul in Acts*. Library of Pauline Studies. Peabody, MA: Hendrickson, 2001.

Schnabel, Eckhard J. *Paul the Missionary: Realities, Strategies, and Methods*. Downers Grove, IL: IVP Academic, 2008.

Schreiner, Thomas R. *Interpreting the Pauline Epistles*. Guides to New Testament Exegesis. Grand Rapids, MI: Baker Book House, 1990.

Thompson, Alan J. *The Acts of the Risen Lord Jesus: Luke's Account of God's Unfolding Plan*. Downers Grove, IL: InterVarsity Press, 2011.